CHRISTIAN DEV

THE
POWER
OF
GOD'S WORD

FOR
OVERCOMING HINDRANCES
TO HEALING

VOLUME 3

A CHRISTIAN DEVOTIONAL
WITH PRAYERS FOR HEALING
AND SCRIPTURES FOR HEALING

BY ANNE B. BUCHANAN

Disclaimer / Limitations of Liability

All material in this book is for information and educational purposes only. No information concerning matters of health is intended as a means to diagnose or treat diseases. No information is intended to be a substitute for medical advice by a licensed health care provider. All readers should consult a licensed health care provider and The Great Physician in all matters relating to medical problems, especially in matters of diagnosing or treating diseases or other physical and mental conditions. The Author and Publisher do not directly or indirectly give medical advice, nor do they prescribe any supplements or assume any responsibility or liability for those who treat themselves. No statements in this publication have been analyzed or approved by the FDA.

Dedicated

To The Glory of God
Who Loves Us
And Who Heals Us

In Memory of
My mother, Elizabeth

TABLE OF CONTENTS

SECTION TWO
Hindrances That Come From
Following The Traditions Of Men

SECTION FOUR
Hindrances That Come From
Not Taking God At His Word

Great Resources

✝
PREFACE

This is Volume 3 of *The Power of God's Word* Series. Our focus in this book is to examine hindrances that keep us from receiving the healing that Jesus has given us through His death on the cross. People sometimes find themselves "stuck" when they stand on the Word of God for their healing. I examine here what many of these hindrances are and how to overcome them.

I have divided the hindrances into four basic categories. They are barriers that come from:

1 – Misunderstanding Scripture
2 – Following traditions of men
3 – Emotional issues
4 – Not taking God at His Word.

Remember that the foundations for many of the Biblical principles that I discuss in these devotions were laid in Volume 1, *The Power of God's Word for Healing,* and also in Volume 2, *The Power of God's Word for Receiving Healing.* Therefore, you will get the most out of this book if you have read those books first. It is especially important that you have read Volume 1 because that book gives the vital keys you must know in order to press through to victory over sickness.

For example, in this book I assume from the beginning that you believe that it is God's will for you to be well. I also assume that you believe that Jesus took every sickness upon Himself and that by His stripes you are healed. If you are not in agreement or you have questions about these two principles, please refer to *The Power of God's Word for Healing*, Volume 1 and *The Power of God's Word for Receiving Healing*, Volume 2 for a thorough explanation.

Volume 3 continues our exploration of the question that used to bother me a lot: "If God is a healer, then why am I sick?" Some people got well. Some did not. Deep in my heart, I just could not accept that it was God's will to heal some people and not others – especially when I seemed to be in the "not others" category.

One of major turning points for me came when I learned the meaning of the Greek word "*sozo*," which is translated "save" in English. Because I did not know the Greek language, I always missed the full impact of what the Holy Spirit was saying in numerous Scriptures. Once I was introduced to the *Strong's Concordance* and I could examine any word in the Bible, an entirely new level of revelation opened up to me.

The Greek word "*sozo*" means "to save, heal, deliver, and make whole." Therefore, it expresses far more than the English translation, "save," conveys. I went through the New Testament and searched for every place where I saw the word "save." I looked in my concordance to see if the Greek word was "*sozo*," and, if so, I wrote the full meaning of the word in the margin of my Bible. When I re-read the passage of Scripture using the full meaning, I was astonished at the message that God was telling me.

I am sharing that revelation with you in this book and hope that it will be as uplifting and illuminating for you as it has been for me. In this book you will learn about God's healing power and how to be made whole through the precious blood of Jesus. It is all about learning what Jesus *really* did for us on the Cross and how to exercise the authority He won for us.

In my own personal life, I find that God's Word and God's remedies make a powerful combination for healing. The God who created me also created the plants, herbs, and essential oils, and I believe He did so with full *intention* – knowing exactly how my body works and how these natural substances meet my bodily needs. However, I want to emphasize that I never forget that it is the Creator who is to be exalted, not the creation. It is the Lord God Almighty who is my Healer, rather than any substance which I may use temporarily to assist my bodily functions to return to a proper balance.

Each person has to take full responsibility for his own health and make his own personal decision about medical care. Those who are on medications need to be particularly cautious. Some medications create a serious physical dependency in the natural world and to discontinue them suddenly can lead to rapid death unless God intervenes supernaturally. God's Word tells us we are not to tempt Him.

Therefore, to discontinue any medication in a rush of "instant faith" would most likely be a fatal decision that would delight the evil one. Don't do it. Instead, strengthen your faith, pray with your medical counselors, and seek God's instruction and your doctor's instructions about what changes to make and when to make them. I am not a medical doctor and do not prescribe or suggest any medical treatments. Please heed the disclaimer at the beginning of this book and seek appropriate health care professionals in matters concerning your health.

Please note that I have taken a few liberties with the English language in this book. I have bent a few rules of grammar so that what you read matches the way that people speak. I have also intentionally spelled satan's name with a small "s" except at the beginning of a sentence. Writing his name in lower case provides a visual reminder that he has been totally defeated by our Risen Savior and has only the power we choose to give him.

This book proclaims God's healing power in small daily doses, boosting our faith step by step and reminding us of God's Holy Word and His covenant with us. It is easy to talk about faith and quite another to navigate the path of healing with focus and purpose. I hope that all who read these messages will be blessed by them.

At the end of the book are a few selected references to materials which you may find useful if you wish to explore further. I am very grateful for those who have long proclaimed God's healing message and who have been instrumental in helping me along the way.

If you like this volume of *The Power of God's Word*, please check out the other volumes in the series, which are available in paperback, on Kindle, and on Nook. Audiobooks are available from amazon.com, iTunes.com, and audible.com. In addition, there are full sets of Scripture cards available. Complete ordering information is on my website: PowerofGodsWord.com.

If you need personal prayer and support, please join our community of believers at our blog website which has many resources available. You will find great articles on numerous topics related to healing, tutorials on free online Bible search websites, videos of healing testimonies, and more.

Share your questions, thoughts, and victories with us and get support for your own journey in healing in a safe environment of like-minded believers. You will find us at: Godwantsyoutobewell.com

Many blessings to each one of you,

Anne Buchanan

P.S. If you like this book, it would be a great blessing to me if you would go to amazon.com and leave a review in the "Customer Reviews" section. Thank you.

SECTION ONE

HINDRANCES THAT COME FROM MISUNDERSTANDING SCRIPTURE

Misunderstanding
and misinterpreting Scripture
can raise many doubts
and severely damage your faith walk.

THE POWER OF GOD'S WORD FOR OVERCOMING

†

DAY 1
WHAT REALLY HAPPENED TO JOB?

And it was so, when the days of their feasting were gone about, that Job sent and sanctified them, and rose up early in the morning, and offered burnt offerings according to the number of them all: for Job said, It may be that my sons have sinned, and cursed God in their hearts. Thus did Job continually. (Job 1:5)

Hast thou not made an hedge about him, and about his house, and about all that he hath on every side? (Job 1:10)

And the Lord said unto Satan, Behold, all that he hath is in thy power; only upon himself put not forth thine hand. So Satan went forth from the presence of the Lord. (Job 1:12)

For the thing which I greatly feared is come upon me, and that which I was afraid of is come unto me. (Job 3:25)

Let's begin with the Bible account of Job because it is often used to show that God inflicts sickness and catastrophe on people – or at least He allows it in order to test people. This story, as it is traditionally interpreted, is quite unsettling. It tells of a good man who followed God, and yet God apparently turned him over to satan and all kinds of awful things happened to him. But we need to take another look at what the Scripture really says.

First of all, notice verse 5, which has critical information for you. It says that Job was extremely concerned about the behavior of his children. He was a godly man himself, but he was constantly worried that his children were not acting in ways that were pleasing to the God. He thought they might be cursing God during their parties, so he kept making sacrifices repeatedly in their behalf. He was now fear-based instead of faith-based. Can you see that?

Satan has been watching Job, and he hates the fact that Job is so blessed and so prosperous. He goes to God and complains. "Have you not made an hedge [of protection] about him, and about his house, and about all that he has on every side?" Just imagine a hedge of protection around you, your family, and everything you have. What was Job like inside that wall? Was he sick? No, he was healthy within God's hedge of protection. Was he poor? No, he was extremely prosperous. Was he toiling to survive? No, he lived under God's blessings.

What happened to the wall? The traditional interpretation is that God removed it. But look at what the Scripture really says. God said to satan, "Look, everything Job has is already in your power" (Job 1:12). Why was that true? Because Job had removed himself from the hedge of protection by his failure to trust God. He was living in constant fear, and he kept acting on that fear. Therefore, he gave satan access to attack him by his own actions.

Later he acknowledged this when he said, "For the thing which I greatly feared is come upon me, and that which I was afraid of is come unto me." (Job 3:25)

As Christians, we have a covenant that Job did not have. Jesus is our hedge of protection! He became the curse for us, and He took every sickness and disease. The satan who attacked Job was a disgraced angel, but he had not been defeated. Satan today is a defeated foe. Jesus went into hell for us, and he defeated the devil and every demonic spirit. They are all defeated.

The Word says that we now have authority over the enemy. Jesus has won that victory for us, and it is up to us to bind every attack of the enemy and to command the devil to leave us. We should never be the victims of satan as Job was. Not ever.

Almighty God, I have authority that Job didn't have because I have the blood and the name of Jesus with which to bind every attack of the enemy. I will not weaken the hedge of protection You have provided, but I will be vigilant instead to keep it strong. Thank You for Your mercy on me and Your tender love. In the name of Your Son, Jesus Christ, I pray, Amen.

✝

DAY 2
JOB TELLS US THE ANSWER HIMSELF

Teach me, and I will hold my tongue: and cause me to understand wherein I have erred.   (Job 6:24)

Thou shalt also decree a thing, and it shall be established unto thee: and the light shall shine upon thy ways.   (Job 22:28)

Neither have I gone back from the commandment of his lips; I have esteemed the words of his mouth more than my necessary food.   (Job 23:12)

Who is he that hideth counsel without knowledge? therefore have I uttered that I understood not; things too wonderful for me, which I knew not.   (Job 42:3)

And the Lord turned the captivity of Job, when he prayed for his friends: also the Lord gave Job twice as much as he had before. (Job 42:10)

Let's finish the vital life lesson that Job gives us. We have seen that Job's fear moved him out from under God's protective covering.

What has happened to your own wall of protection? Have you, or those from whom you are descended, removed it? With choice after choice, have you removed your protective wall one brick at a time? Jesus died to give us the protective covering of His precious blood. But we have to stay firmly rooted in faith in order to receive the benefits of that covering. If we indulge in fear, we too move ourselves out from under His protection.

Job realized that it was his tongue that was the problem. He was speaking fear instead of speaking faith. He had to learn to change his thoughts and his words. He said, "Teach me, and I will hold my tongue: and cause me to understand wherein I have erred" (Job 6:24). We must do the same.

The Word goes on to say that what we decree with our mouth will be established in our lives. Too often we talk our fears when we don't understand how damaging that is to our faith. We have to develop the attitude that Job came to have so that we "esteem the words of God's mouth more than our necessary food." (Job 23:12). God's Word is the key, and we have to insure that our words agree with God's Words.

What happened to Job in the end when he finally understood what had happened? God had mercy on him and restored to him double what he had had previously.

No matter what you may have done in the past, God wants to redeem you. He has released His healing power and He wants you to receive it and be made whole. Your course is ever the same – to stand faithfully on God's Word and to trust in Jehovah-Rapha, the God who heals you.

Father God, I am sorry that I have spoken fears and doubts that are contrary to Your Holy Word. I realize that, if I decree a thing, it will be established for me. I repent of things I have decreed in the past that I do not want to happen, Father. I thank You for forgiving me of those mistakes, and I am so grateful that You wipe them away to give me a fresh start. I do esteem Your Words more than my food, and I am determined to spend more time meditating on Your Word to get it deep in my heart. I thank You for the gift of Your precious Son, Jesus, and for restoring my health, my finances, my relationships, and all Your marvelous blessings. In Jesus' mighty name, I pray, Amen.

†

DAY 3
WAS PAUL'S THORN SICKNESS?

And lest I should be exalted above measure through the abundance of the revelations, there was given to me a thorn in the flesh, the messenger of Satan to buffet me, lest I should be exalted above measure.   (2 Corinthians 12:7)

Now let's tackle the issue of Paul's "thorn in the flesh." Many people use this passage in 2 Corinthians as an argument that God not only does not always heal but that He actually makes us sick for some purpose of His own. They believe Paul had eye trouble or some other ailment which God refused to heal.

The use of the word "thorn" as a figurative example of a problem occurs in the Bible in the Old Testament. We find it in Numbers 33:55 and also in Joshua 23:13. Even today we refer to a problematic person as being a "thorn in our side." In this letter to the Corinthians, Paul uses it similarly, and he does not mean a literal physical illness or thing.

Paul tells us exactly what the thorn is: it is a messenger of satan. The Greek word that Paul used is *"angelos,"* which appears numerous times usually translated "angel" and occasionally translated "messenger." It is a personality that is his problem, not a thing such as illness. While some translations read that Paul asked God to take "it" (meaning the thorn) away from him, a translation by Weymouth says, "... I besought the Lord to rid me of him." The thorn was one of satan's cohorts, coming at Paul repeatedly.

Paul wanted God to stop the demonic attacks that kept coming at him relentlessly - shipwrecks, imprisonment, beatings, etc. However, until the devil is finally sent to hell forever, God is not going to stop him from his activity. What He has done is to defeat satan and given us authority to deal with him. This is hard work, and Paul was tired. He wanted God to get the devil off his case. God basically told Paul (if I may take a few liberties with Ephesians 3:20), "The ball is in your court. You use the tools I have given you. You are weak on your own, but I have given you dynamite power that works in you."

The firmer you become in your faith and the more strongly you are willing to follow the Lord God Almighty, the more likely satan is to come after you. But God has provided. He says to you, "My grace is sufficient for you, for my power is made perfect in weakness."

Almighty God, thank You for the armor of protection that You have given me. When the evil one tries to buffet me as he did Paul, I resist Him in Your name and in the name of Your Son, Jesus Christ, who defeated Him fully for all of time. Your grace is sufficient for me, and Your power is made perfect in my weakness. Through the blood of Jesus, I walk in total victory, and, therefore, I rejoice! In Jesus' name, I pray, Amen.

✝

DAY 4
WHAT WAS PAUL'S INFIRMITY
OF THE FLESH?

Ye know how through infirmity of the flesh I preached the gospel unto you at the first. And my temptation which was in my flesh ye despised not, nor rejected; but received me as an angel of God, even as Christ Jesus. Where is then the blessedness ye spake of? for I bear you record, that, if it had been possible, ye would have plucked out your own eyes, and have given them to me. (Galatians 4:13-15)

Paul clearly writes to the Galatians that he had some kind of "infirmity of the flesh" when he first preached to them. Was he saying that he had eye trouble that was never healed? If the answer is yes, then can you still have assurance that God wants you to be well?

Let's turn to Acts 14 to see what Paul is talking about. "And there came thither certain Jews from Antioch and Iconium, who persuaded the people, and, having stoned Paul, drew him out of the city, supposing he had been dead. Howbeit, as the disciples stood round about him, he rose up, and came into the city: and the next day he departed with Barnabas to Derbe." (Acts 14:19-20)

From this account we find out that Paul was stoned by the Jews in Lystra (a fact that he mentions in 2 Corinthians 11:25). Some scholars believe that Paul actually died and then was raised from the dead by his disciples.

Whether he died or not, we don't know. But we do know that everyone thought he was dead. The believers with him surrounded him and certainly prayed for him, and he rose up. The next day he departed to the city of Derbe which was 15 to 20 miles away.

He did what? Here he was stoned so badly everyone thought he was dead. But he rose up and the very next day traveled at least 15 miles to preach in Derbe. When is the last time you walked 15 miles in one day? Remember there were no cars, no trains, not even any bicycles. Travel was either by foot, horse, or cart. If Paul's miraculous healing was not one hundred percent completed instantaneously, do you suppose he might have still had bruises, injuries, and discomfort the next morning?

So he says in Galatians that "through infirmity of the flesh I preached the gospel unto you at the first." Notice the information in that one sentence. He was still feeling the effects of his near-fatal stoning that had occurred just before he went to Derbe. Nevertheless, he was clearly able to preach and minister. And lastly, he stayed there for a while and the people were kind to him during his recovery.

The implication is that he was recovered by the time that he left. God never wants us to stay injured. It is always His plan to heal.

So this account of Paul's recovery has a glorious message for us. God wants us to be well, and through the death and resurrection of Jesus, He has provided for us to receive His healing power. Take it now because it is yours!

Father God, thank You for the encouragement of the Word that shows me in great detail that You are my healer. You love me as much as You loved Paul, so I receive Your healing power now. If Paul can overcome being stoned, then I can overcome this attack of the enemy against my body. I declare and decree that I am healed in Jesus' name! And it is in His name that I pray, Amen.

†

Day 5
Did Paul Have a Problem With His Eyes?

Ye know how through infirmity of the flesh I preached the gospel unto you at the first.

And my temptation which was in my flesh ye despised not, nor rejected; but received me as an angel of God, even as Christ Jesus.

Where is then the blessedness ye spake of? for I bear you record, that, if it had been possible, ye would have plucked out your own eyes, and have given them to me. (Galatians 4:13-15)

Let's continue taking a look at the issue of Paul's eyesight. Paul thanked the Galatians for their willingness to "have plucked out your own eyes" for him.

One explanation is that something was wrong with Paul's eyes and the believers would have been glad to have given him their own eyes. Some translations of the Bible use words to that effect.

Remember that Paul had just been stoned nearly to death. Many large stones were thrown on his head, so it is possible that for the next few days his eyesight was affected. Do we know for certain? The answer to that is no.

Scripture does not describe the nature of Paul's injuries from the stoning, so we can only speculate. And speculation is not truth. All we know is that injury to his eyes from the stoning is a possibility. What we do know by Paul's own testimony is that the problem existed *only at the beginning* of his time in Derbe, and therefore, his healing was complete by the time that he left.

Is there another way to look at the words "you would have plucked out your own eyes"? As a matter of fact, there is.

Have you ever been in an intense situation and said something like, "I'd give my right arm if my son could hit a home run in the championship game"? Do you mean that your son couldn't play in the game because he was lacking an arm, so you would gladly give him your arm? Of course not. You are using a figure of speech to illustrate your love, your concern, and your great desire to help him.

In a similar way, it is just as likely that Paul was using a figure of speech here to describe the loving care of the Galatians for him rather than indicating a precise physical injury.

We don't know which meaning Paul intended to share. But again, I will repeat the statement I made above. What we do know by Paul's own testimony is that the problem (whatever it was) existed only at the beginning of his time in Derbe, and therefore his healing was complete by the time that he left.

Use Paul's example to strengthen your faith for your own healing.

Father God, thank You for Paul's example to me. He was injured so badly that everyone thought he was dead. Yet Your healing power flowed to him so that he was able to get up, travel 15 miles to the next town, preach, minister, and do Your work the very next day. I declare the same healing power of the blood of Jesus over the attacks on my body. Like Paul, I receive my healing and move forward to fulfill the purpose You have for my life. In Jesus' name, I pray, Amen.

✝

Day 6
What About Paul's Handwriting?

Ye see how large a letter I have written unto you with mine own hand.   (Galatians 6:11)

Before we leave the topic of Paul's eyesight, there is one more Scripture to consider. That is Paul's comment at the end of the letter to the Galatians, which reads in the *King James Version*, "Ye see how large a letter I have written unto you with mine own hand."

The *New International Version* says, "See what large letters I use as I write to you with my own hand!" *The Message* translates, "Now, in these last sentences, I want to emphasize in the bold scrawls of my personal handwriting the immense importance of what I have written to you."

You can see that the English words do not mean the same thing at all. Do we accept the *King James Version* which seems to be referring to the fact that the letter to the Galatians was a long letter written by Paul? Or do we rely on the *New International Version* which implies that Paul had to write using very big letters that were somehow unusual for him? Or do we lean on *The Message* which says that Paul is writing in a big, bold scrawl which was apparently normal for him?

We do know that Paul had had a problem with people forging letters under his name, so he was making clear to the Galatians that this letter was truly from him and not someone else.

The real issue in examining these translations is what difference they make in your beliefs. There is clearly no agreement among Greek scholars as to the accurate translation of this verse. Are you going to build an entire theology around the particular version you are reading?

The differences among these translations reminds us that God ordained that the New Testament be originally written in Greek. It would be wonderful if each of us could learn that marvelous language so that we could receive God's Words without the challenges of translation. But most of us will never be Greek scholars or linguists.

So what are you supposed to do when you find such differences in translations? Go to the Holy Spirit who is your teacher and guide and ask Him to reveal His truth to you. He will show you and bring peace to your mind and heart.

Heavenly Father, confusion does not come from You, so I ask for revelation knowledge through the Holy Spirit about this verse of Scripture. You have given me verse after verse after verse proclaiming Your covenant that You are the God who heals. Help me to remove every doubt so that I can walk in the fullness of Your healing power. In Jesus' name, I pray, Amen.

✝

DAY 7
WHAT WERE PAUL'S INFIRMITIES?

... Most gladly therefore will I rather glory in my infirmities, that the power of Christ may rest upon me.

Therefore I take pleasure in infirmities, in reproaches, in necessities, in persecutions, in distresses for Christ's sake: for when I am weak, then am I strong.   (2 Corinthians 12:9-10)

Many people are confused by Paul's repeated use of the word "infirmities" in these verses because they believe that Paul is saying that he gloried in having health problems. What did he mean?

As always, we have to look at the Greek. Strong's Concordance tells us that the Greek word for "infirmities" is "*astheneia,*" which means feebleness of body or mind, weakness, frailty, disease, sickness, malady, or infirmity.

That does not settle the issue since we see that the word can refer either to a condition of weakness or a physical problem. We still do not know which meaning Paul had in mind. When this happens, we have to dig deeper.

Let's look at other uses of the same word. Hebrews 4:15 says, "For we have not an high priest which cannot be touched with the feeling of our infirmities; but was in all points tempted like as we are, yet without sin." Are infirmities sicknesses here? Clearly not. What about

Hebrews 7:28: "For the law maketh men high priests which have infirmity; but the word of the oath, which was since the law, maketh the Son, who is consecrated for evermore." Here again infirmity is weakness rather than physical illness.

This tells us that we have to look at the context in order to determine the meaning. Remember that Paul did not write his letter using chapter or verse designations.

If we go back to 2 Corinthians 11:23-30, Paul gives us an extremely long list of difficulties including stoning, beatings, shipwreck, hunger, treachery, fatigue, and the cares of all the churches. He says, "Who is weak, and I am not weak? Who is offended, and I burn not? If I must needs glory, I will glory of the things which concern mine infirmities." Here is that same word "infirmities" again.

Paul himself has clearly categorized all his troubles by using the Greek word *"astheneia,"* which we now know was translated "infirmities" in English. Now let's look again at the list Paul just gave us in which he describes for us what he considers "infirmities" to be. Is sickness anywhere on his very, very long list? No. Not once. There is no mention of any health problem whatsoever.

We need to take Paul at his word. He carefully listed his problems, called them infirmities, and continued the same train of thought into his discussion about the attacks of satan. Look at God's Word with new eyes and see the truth that tells you over and over that God wants you well.

Father God, thank You for giving me new revelation about Your Holy Word. Help me to study Your Word to learn Your truth and

Your will that You want me healthy and well. Thank You for giving me revelation, understanding, and wisdom so that I can build a strong faith on Your truth, Your goodness, and Your love. In Jesus' name, I pray, Amen

✝

DAY 8
WHY WAS PAUL'S ASSISTANT SICK?

Erastus abode at Corinth: but Trophimus have I left at Miletum sick. (2 Timothy 4:20)

Certain Scriptures raise questions in people's minds whether it is God's will to heal everyone. This is one of those passages that leads some people to doubt.

Acts 20 describes a portion of Paul's journeys in which he had gone to Greece for three months. He then left to continue his missionary journey, spreading the gospel and strengthening the early Christian communities. Several people are named who traveled with him and one of them was Trophimus (Acts 20:4).

Eventually the group reached the city of Miletus. Nothing is said in the account in Acts about Trophimus becoming ill, but Paul mentions in his letter to Timothy that he had to go on, leaving Trophimus behind because he was sick.

Some people say, "If Paul couldn't get his own helper healed, then that proves that God doesn't always heal people." This is a faulty conclusion, and it is one that can block your receiving your healing.

In the first place, Trophimus did not stay sick. In Acts 21, Paul is in Jerusalem and Trophimus is with him.

"For they had seen before with him in the city Trophimus, an Ephesian, whom they supposed that Paul had brought into the temple" (Acts 21:29). Whatever his problem was, he had recovered. Not everyone receives his healing instantaneously, so Trophimus may have needed to stay behind until his healing was fully manifested.

Another explanation is that working with or for a person who walks in great revelation of the Word does not guarantee that you will walk in the same revelation. Each one of us has to establish our own faith. We can receive a healing based largely on someone else's faith once or twice, but eventually we have to find it for ourselves.

The important thing to remember is that Trophimus did recover and did continue to work with Paul in spreading the Gospel of the Lord Jesus Christ, who died to save, deliver, and heal us.

Father God, I thank You for teachers who share their revelation of Your Holy Word with me. I am grateful for the insight that they share, opening for me new understanding of Your Word. They show me truths that I have missed and encourage my faith. I want to deepen my relationship with You so that I can walk in the fullness of every blessing You have for me. I know that Your healing power flows to me every moment of every day. I receive it, Father, and I give You all the glory. In Jesus' name, I pray, Amen.

✝

Day 9
What Is Suffering?

... And we rejoice in the hope of the glory of God.

Not only so, but we also rejoice in our sufferings, because we know that suffering produces perseverance; perseverance, character; and character, hope. (Romans 5:2-4 *New International Version*)

These verses are often used as a justification of God-authored illness and of the need to endure our physical ailments. For those who believe that God wants His children to be well, how can we be reconciled to this Scripture? We have to look at the meaning of the word that is translated "suffering" in English.

The Greek word in these verses that is translated "sufferings" is "*thlipsis*." "*Thlipsis*" generally means trouble, distress, oppression, and tribulation – none of which refers automatically to suffering from illness. This Greek word usually conveys the sense of a terrible pressure or a crushing burden. The devil comes at us with load after load after load – all designed to destroy and kill us.

Jesus told His followers plainly that they would be subject to trials and tribulations. "Then shall they deliver you up to be afflicted, and shall kill you: and ye shall be hated of all nations for my name's sake" (Matthew 24:9).

He also said, "These things I have spoken unto you, that in me ye might have peace. In the world ye shall have tribulation: but be of good cheer; I have overcome the world" (John 16:33).

In His own life Jesus encountered many difficulties, and He had to overcome many attempts of oppression. He was constantly harassed by those in authority, and they repeatedly plotted against Him until the time came when He allowed them to arrest, beat, and crucify Him.

Jesus is our perfect example of how to handle life. He knew what it was to suffer persecution and attack. But it is interesting that none of His sufferings involved personal sickness and disease until He bore them on the Cross.

Yes, Jesus was the Son of God. But He came in a human body for a reason. He came in a body precisely to show us how to live in it and how to treat it as a precious temple of the Holy Spirit.

Jesus knew what it was like to be weak from hunger and thirst. He knew what it was like to be so tired that He had to get away from everyone and lie down. If He had not lived in a human body like the rest of us, we could not relate to Him so personally and so intensely.

God sent Jesus to show us the way. "I am the way," He told us. He was then and still is now.

Almighty God, I declare like Paul that I rejoice in tribulations that come as a result of my proclaiming Your Word and standing for Your truth at times when it's not easy or popular. Through these trials I learn perseverance, develop character, and strengthen hope.

I know that physical suffering is not Your will for me and that Your Son, Jesus Christ, has overcome every illness and every disease. I rejoice in knowing that I live triumphantly in the victory that Jesus won for me on the Cross. In Jesus' name, I pray, Amen.

✝

DAY 10
DOES SUFFERING GLORIFY GOD?

... if so be that we suffer with him, that we may be also glorified together. For I reckon that the sufferings of this present time are not worthy to be compared with the glory which shall be revealed in us. (Romans 8:17-18)

How many people have died before their time by believing that Romans 8 was telling them that suffering from their illness was somehow glorifying God? They misunderstand that the sufferings Paul is speaking of are trials and tribulations coming because of the Gospel and are not sickness and disease coming from an attack of the enemy.

In the previous devotion on Day 9, we saw that the English word "suffering" (used in Romans 5) came from the Greek word "*thlipsis*," which meant trouble, distress, oppression, and tribulation, or a crushing burden. In the verse in today's devotion (in Romans 8) we find the same English word of "suffer" and "sufferings." However, the Apostle Paul used different Greek words to convey a slightly different meaning.

The word "suffer" is the Greek word "*sumpascho*" – from which we get the English word "sympathy." It means "to experience feelings jointly." The word "sufferings" is the Greek word "*pathema*," which means "something

51

THE POWER OF GOD'S WORD FOR OVERCOMING

undergone, such as an emotion, hardship, or pain." Do you see that Paul is not talking about sickness and disease here?

Notice the phrase "suffer *with* him." This does not say we suffer *for* Jesus, but that we suffer *with* Jesus – or are joined with Him. If we misinterpret this verse and insist on saying that we are suffering physical pain of disease *for* Jesus, that would deny what Jesus did for us on the Cross.

Jesus is the One who took our sicknesses and diseases on Himself and suffered them *for us* on the Cross. If we turn around and say we are doing that same thing for Him, then we are saying Jesus did not quite finish the job. And make no mistake about it. *It is finished.* Jesus completed the job perfectly, and He sits at the right hand of the Father so that we can walk in the victory He died to give us.

People also miss the little phrase "in us." Paul says that he reckons that the hardships (the "sufferings") of this present time are not worthy to be compared with the glory which shall be revealed *in us*. He did not say that the sufferings of this present time are not worthy to be compared with the glory which shall be revealed *to us* at a later time in heaven. No one suffers cancer now because it is not worthy to be compared with the glory that will be revealed to them when they soon get to heaven. That is an incorrect interpretation.

We are supposed to be walking in the victory won by Jesus on the Cross. Paul is saying, "You know, the trials I'm going through right now aren't worthy to be compared with the glory that is being revealed today (and every day in the future) in me and through me."

You can see this belief reflected in the prayers that he prayed for other Christians (especially Ephesians 1:16-23). Read them carefully. He says, "I pray for you to have revelation of knowledge of Him. Knowledge. Wisdom. Judgment. Discernment. Sincerity. Allowing the power of God to work through you." Those things are the glory that is being revealed.

Jesus came to give you victory. Seek revelation knowledge of everything that is included in the atonement – healing, salvation, deliverance, and wholeness.

Father God, give me a spirit of wisdom and revelation in the knowledge of Your Son, Jesus. I am joined with Jesus so that I may be also glorified together with Him. I know that the pressures of this present time are not worthy to be compared with the glory which You are revealing in me. I ask for understanding and discernment so that Your power can work through me for Your glory. In Jesus' name, I pray, Amen.

✝

Day 11
Do All Things Work Together
For Your Good?

And He Who searches the hearts of men knows what is in the mind of the [Holy] Spirit [what His intent is], because the Spirit intercedes and pleads [before God] in behalf of the saints according to and in harmony with God's will.

We are assured and know that [God being a partner in their labor] all things work together and are [fitting into a plan] for good to and for those who love God and are called according to [His] design and purpose.   (Romans 8:27-28   Amplified Bible)

Sometimes people use this verse of Scripture interchangeably with the statement that "God has a reason for giving me this disease or accident or problem." They assume that the phrase "all things work together for good" means that *everything that happens to them* is an act of God's will. Consequently, people don't resist satan and his destructive acts but actually declare them to be some mysterious act of God.

This confusion comes from removing the sentence from its context. Note that Paul is talking about the effects of intercessory prayer which the Holy Spirit is making for the saints. Prayers are being offered by the Holy Spirit according to and in harmony with God's will. Nothing is being prayed for that is not according to God's will. We are now assured that, *whenever God is a partner,* all things work together for good for those who love Him. This interpretation makes perfect sense.

Do things happen to people that were not intended for their good? Absolutely, yes. Satan is not working for your good. Satan is trying to destroy you, to kill you, and to steal your health, finances, relationships, and joy. Many things may happen to you that are caused completely by the enemy.

Attributing every event in your life to God is to deny satan's existence. It is written that satan creeps around like a lion looking for prey. Some of the easiest pickings are those who believe that everything that happens in their life is planned by God.

God has made it clear that people can choose between good and evil, between life and death, between Him and the devil. You have that choice a thousand times a day, and so does everyone else. God even tells you the answer: choose good, choose life, and choose Him.

The good news is that evil cannot win when we choose to follow the Lord God Almighty because Jesus has overcome satan. No matter how satan attacks you, no matter what illness or accident may befall you, the victory over it has already been won by Jesus Christ.

God can create good out of any situation, no matter how badly it may have begun. God can turn any situation around. God can bring order from chaos, victory from the jaws of defeat, and life from death.

If you have fallen into a trap of the enemy, do not give up. God has given you the tools to take authority and to speak victory over your situation. He is pouring out His mercy, grace, and healing in great abundance, and He wants you to rise up as a testimony to His great love. So stand in the authority that God has given you and trust Him completely with your life.

Father, You know everything that I need. I ask the Holy Spirit to intercede for me in harmony with Your divine will. I am assured that, when You are my partner, all things coming from You work together for my good. Thank You, Father, for healing me. In Jesus' name, Amen.

✝

DAY 12
DO YOU BELIEVE ALL OF
THE GREAT COMMISSION?

And he said unto them, Go ye into all the world, and preach the gospel to every creature. He that believeth and is baptized shall be saved; but he that believeth not shall be damned [condemned]. And these signs shall follow them that believe; In my name shall they cast out devils; they shall speak with new tongues; They shall take up serpents; and if they drink any deadly thing, it shall not hurt them; they shall lay hands on the sick, and they shall recover. (Mark 16:15-18)

When most people quote the Great Commission of Jesus, they stop at the end of the first sentence. They say, "Go ye into all the world, and preach the gospel to every creature." A few people will go on to quote the second sentence, but almost everyone stops there. However, Jesus went on to say some very profound and important things in verses 17 and 18.

First, you have to settle for yourself the issue of the authenticity of this passage of Scripture. Some early Greek manuscripts have a shorter ending of chapter 16 that adds a couple of sentences to verse 8 and then stops there. Other manuscripts have the longer ending that we have in the King James Version. You have to decide whether you believe the Holy Spirit directed men to include verses 9 through 20. What you believe will determine what you will manifest in your life. I have decided to believe and trust in the longer version. One main reason is that I see evidence in the lives of the Apostles of their implementing these instructions in their lives.

Jesus says that several signs that will "follow them that believe." That means me and that means you. We are "them that believe." The list starts out with casting out devils (which we see Paul do in Acts 16:16-18) and speaking in new tongues (which we see in Acts 2:4 and elsewhere). Especially troublesome to most people are the next items in the list about "taking up snakes" and "drinking any deadly thing." At this point many people decide to disregard the entire set of verses because they are confused.

This is unfortunate both because those instructions are valid and because people then miss one of the most powerful statements in the Bible. "They shall lay hands on the sick, and they shall recover." What a magnificent statement from the Lord!

Please remember the instructions that Jesus gave to His disciples during His three years of ministry. In Matthew 10:8, we read this: "Heal the sick, cleanse the lepers, raise the dead, cast out devils: freely ye have received, freely give."

Some people turn that verse into a discussion on freely giving money. But Jesus wasn't talking about money. He was talking about healing the sick and casting out demons and raising the dead. These are things most people do not think they can do today. They do not think it applies to them because somehow we are stuck in a less powerful situation than the early believers were. That is simply not true.

Jesus has commanded all of us to go as His disciples into all the world, spreading the gospel and healing those who are ill. He knew that He was sending us into all kinds of locations and situations throughout the world. He needed to assure us that we could walk in His protective care. He tells us that, if we truly believe, we will be protected. Let's have the courage to obey Jesus' commands and be His instruments for healing.

Almighty Lord, I accept the Great Commission of Your Son, Jesus Christ. I choose to believe what is in the Word of God in Mark 16:15-20. Therefore, Father, I commit myself to share Jesus' message of the kingdom of heaven, to deliver those in bondage to the enemy, and to lay hands on the sick so that they will recover. I thank You that other believers are empowered by You to lay hands on me so that I can manifest my full recovery. I give You grateful thanks and in Jesus' name, I pray, Amen.

✝

DAY 13
TAKING UP SERPENTS

And the barbarous people showed us no little kindness: for they kindled a fire, and received us every one, because of the present rain, and because of the cold.

And when Paul had gathered a bundle of sticks, and laid them on the fire, there came a viper out of the heat, and fastened on his hand. And when the barbarians saw the venomous beast hang on his hand, they said among themselves, No doubt this man is a murderer, whom, though he hath escaped the sea, yet vengeance suffereth not to live.

And he shook off the beast into the fire, and felt no harm. Howbeit they looked when he should have swollen, or fallen down dead suddenly: but after they had looked a great while, and saw no harm come to him, they changed their minds, and said that he was a god.   (Acts 28:2-6)

Let's take a look at the matter of "taking up serpents." Some scholars believe that the term "serpents" in Mark 16:18 is a reference to devils, and that, therefore, Jesus is emphasizing the dominion that Christians are to have over satan. On the other hand, most Greek scholars think that Jesus was referring to real serpents (snakes) in their natural meaning.

Unfortunately, a few people think they are supposed to pick up snakes in church on purpose. They forget that

Jesus refused to jump off the Temple roof when satan dared him. He said "Thou shalt not tempt the Lord thy God" (Matthew 4:7). Surely Jesus would apply the same principle to picking up snakes or drinking poison intentionally just to prove a point.

Fortunately, the Word of God comes to our rescue because it gives an actual illustration of this verse in Acts 28:1-9. Paul had been shipwrecked on the island of Melita and he was stirring the fire when a snake jumped out and bit him. The islanders first reaction was that Paul must be a murderer since the snake bit him and wouldn't let go. It just hung there, latched onto Paul's hand.

Of course, we know that earlier in his life Paul actually had participated in condemning some Christians to death. However, after his dramatic conversion experience on the road to Damascus, he had been forgiven by the Lord, and he became a passionate believer in the Lord Jesus Christ.

Paul was taught by Jesus directly for three years (Galatians 1:11-18), so he knew the commission that Jesus had left for all His followers. Paul believed Jesus meant exactly what He said, so he worked diligently to do as Jesus commanded. Therefore, when the snake bit him, Paul was not afraid because he knew that Jesus had declared His protection in just such circumstances. He simply shook off the snake and kept on doing his chores.

After the islanders saw that Paul didn't die or suffer any ill effects from the snake bite, they then called Paul a god because what they witnessed defied the laws of nature. Paul was not a god, of course, but he had the power of Almighty

God within him, and he had the promises of His Lord and Savior.

What happened next? First he healed the chief's father. How? By following the last command in the list – by the laying on of hands. And what was the result? Exactly what Mark 16 says, "... and they shall recover." Once people witnessed that healing, they brought every sick person on the whole island to Paul and every single one of them was healed. All of them. I repeat, all of them were healed.

God has set laws of nature in action. We are not supposed to tempt God and to violate them on purpose. But we can confess the Word if some accident happens to us, and we can expect to walk in victory just as Paul did.

Look at all the glory and honor for God that came from Paul's encounter with the snake. Paul went on to enforce the command to lay hands on the sick, and he saw that everyone recovered through God's healing power.

You are no different from Paul. Jesus may not have called you as dramatically, but His call is no less real. Are you Paul's kind of Christian who is able to believe without allowing doubt to limit and weaken you? Let the signs of being a Christian accompany you.

Almighty God, I profess my faith in You and in Your Son, Jesus Christ. Let me use Paul's life as an example of what service to You in total faith means. Help me as I strive to be a faithful witness for You. With humility and boldness I declare myself to be a Christian, and I pray that signs and wonders follow me for Your glory. In Jesus' name, I pray, Amen.

✝

DAY 14
IS LAYING ON OF HANDS REAL?

In the same quarters were possessions of the chief man of the island, whose name was Publius; who received us, and lodged us three days courteously.

And it came to pass, that the father of Publius lay sick of a fever and of a bloody flux: to whom Paul entered in, and prayed, and laid his hands on him, and healed him.

So when this was done, others also, which had diseases in the island, came, and were healed.   (Acts 28:7-9)

We will take a closer look at what Paul did on the island of Melita. We have seen that he laid hands on people and they recovered fully. Isn't it sad that some people have turned the laying on of hands into a performance, complete with fake "cures"? Satan never ceases to work to get control, and he is delighted that laying on of hands is now perceived by many people as a kind of bogus hocus-pocus.

The laying on of hands is real. Jesus did it. He taught His disciples to do it. And He told them to teach others to do it. In the Great Commission described in Mark 16:15-20, Jesus instructed all who believe on Him to go into all the world, preach the good news, teach and disciple others, cast out demons, and lay their hands on sick people so they would get well.

Here we see Paul doing exactly that – following Jesus' instructions by going into far countries, preaching the Gospel, training disciples, laying his hands on the sick, and healing them. These actions of obedience were faithfully done by the followers in the early church, but the laying on of hands was gradually done less and less until it is rarely found in the church today.

Paul was not one of Jesus' original disciples. Like us, he was called after Jesus had been crucified, resurrected, and ascended into heaven. In this story Paul was on the island of Melita where, by prayer and the laying on of hands, he healed the island chief's father, who was sick with a fever and dysentery. The word of this healing spread and then everybody else on the island who was sick came to him. Every single one of them was healed, and again we find no exceptions.

The truth is that you are no different from Paul. You have your own strengths, weaknesses, and talents, but Jesus' commission is as valid for you as it was for Paul. It is not a requirement that someone lay hands on you in order for you to be healed, but it is one way that has been given as a method for healing.

And did you know that you can lay hands on yourself for your healing? Well, you can. When you have someone else lay hands on you, then you have the benefit of the prayer of agreement. However, if no one else is available, you can certainly lay hands on your own body and appropriate your healing.

Almighty God, I never paid much attention to the command about the laying on of hands so that the sick would recover. I am sorry that I did not understand that part of Your Word, but thank You for revealing it to me now. Thank You for giving me the example of Paul and showing me not only how I can be prayed for but also how I can pray for others to help them. In the name of Your Son, Jesus Christ, I pray, Amen.

✝

DAY 15
WHEN THE LAYING ON OF HANDS
IS MISUSED

But there was a certain man, called Simon, which beforetime in the same city used sorcery, and bewitched the people of Samaria, giving out that himself was some great one: to whom they all gave heed, from the least to the greatest, saying, This man is the great power of God. And to him they had regard, because that of long time he had bewitched them with sorceries.

But when they believed Philip preaching the things concerning the kingdom of God, and the name of Jesus Christ, they were baptized, both men and women.

Then Simon himself believed also: and when he was baptized, he continued with Philip, and wondered, beholding the miracles and signs which were done.

Now when the apostles which were at Jerusalem heard that Samaria had received the word of God, they sent unto them Peter and John: who, when they were come down, prayed for them, that they might receive the Holy Ghost: (For as yet he was fallen upon none of them: only they were baptized in the name of the Lord Jesus.) Then laid they their hands on them, and they received the Holy Ghost.

And when Simon saw that through laying on of the apostles' hands the Holy Ghost was given, he offered them money, saying, Give me also this power, that on whomsoever I lay hands, he may receive the Holy Ghost.

But Peter said unto him, Thy money perish with thee, because thou hast thought that the gift of God may be purchased with money. Thou hast neither part nor lot in this matter: for thy heart is not right in the sight of God.

Repent therefore of this thy wickedness, and pray God, if perhaps the thought of thine heart may be forgiven thee.   (Acts 8:9-22)

The laying on of hands is used for the healing of the sick, and it is also used for the baptism of the Holy Spirit. A sorcerer named Simon had seen the immediate results when Peter had baptized people with the Holy Spirit by the laying on of hands. He was an expert in various forms of magic, and he had gotten much of his training by paying for it.   That is still true today.   For example, people pay a "master" to learn the New Age method of healing called Reiki.

Even though Simon had been baptized and supposedly gave up sorcery, he offered money to Peter and John so that they could teach him how to baptize others with the Holy Spirit. Peter rebuked him forcefully ("thy money perish with thee") because nothing related to the Holy Spirit – the third person of the Trinity – could ever be bought or sold. The idea Simon had of using the baptism of the Holy Spirit as a tool to manipulate people was from satan and not from God.

Today there are a few people who appear to use laying on of hands when, in fact, they are putting on a performance. Just because a few frauds exist, please do not reject the laying on of hands as a valid means of healing or receiving the baptism of the Holy Spirit. Such a decision can be a big hindrance to your receiving your healing.

Jesus Himself taught us to do it, and in His last words before His ascension, He declared that the laying on of hands for the healing of the sick would be a sign of those who followed Him. The laying on of hands for the healing of the sick is real. It is important. And it is a gift from the Father.

Father God, what a blessed gift the laying on of hands is for me. Through the laying on of hands, the sick recover according to the command of Your Son, Jesus Christ. I am grateful to receive the laying on of hands for my healing, and I am also obedient to lay hands on others as a sign that I am a believer. In Jesus' name, I pray, Amen.

✝

DAY 16
CAN YOU BE HEALED THROUGH A HANDKERCHIEF?

And God wrought special miracles by the hands of Paul: So that from his body were brought unto the sick handkerchiefs or aprons, and the diseases departed from them, and the evil spirits went out of them. (Acts 19:11-12)

We are told in this passage of Holy Scripture that "God wrought special miracles by the hands of Paul." Isn't it an amazing testimony about the redemptive power of God to think that a person who had persecuted and killed many Christians later came to do extraordinary miracles?

What is a miracle? It is a way that God uses to say, "I am here. I am the Lord God Almighty." It is an event that is so contrary to what people believe "ought" to happen that all who witness it recognize that something awesome has occurred.

In most cases when Jesus performed miracles, the response of the people was to glorify the God of Israel. Notice that the writer of Acts does not say that Paul did the miracles, but he specifically says that God did the miracles by using Paul – and the pieces of cloth – as His instruments.

What were these miracles? Paul touched handkerchiefs and aprons, which were taken to sick people and the people recovered. The strong anointing from God transferred to the cloth in a miraculous way. And this is still a valid method for helping someone to engage his faith to receive his healing. Do the handkerchiefs heal? No. But by a God ordained process, cloth has the ability to retain the anointing of God in it. It is the anointing of God that heals.

The healings that occurred through the pieces of cloth that Paul had anointed were complete. Illnesses were cured and demons were expelled. The benefits of the atonement were at work, resulting in healing, deliverance, and total freedom from infirmities and bondage.

Today some people exchange anointed prayer cloths for money, either by selling them outright or by requesting a "love offering" for them. Peter gives us God's view of such a thing. "Thy money perish with thee, because thou hast thought that the gift of God may be purchased with money" (Acts 8:20). But do not let the error of a few make you cynical and unbelieving.

Healing is real. Miracles are real. The anointing through handkerchiefs and cloth is real. God wants us well so that we can testify to the whole world of His love and glory.

Father God, I am filled with awe at Your mighty power. You worked many mighty miracles through the hands of Paul. I want to be a disciple like him, Father, so that You can work through me to show others the awesome benefits of salvation, healing, deliverance, and being made whole. I want to do Your work, using laying on of hands and even the anointing of cloths, as You direct me. Thank You for sending Your Son as my example, and thank

You for giving me Your precious Word to show me how other believers carried on Your mission and plan. In Jesus' name, I pray, Amen.

†

DAY 17
JESUS TOOK OUR SICKNESS

He is despised and rejected of men; a man of sorrows, and acquainted with grief: and we hid as it were our faces from him; he was despised, and we esteemed him not. Surely he hath borne our griefs, and carried our sorrows: yet we did esteem him stricken, smitten of God, and afflicted. But he was wounded for our transgressions, he was bruised for our iniquities: the chastisement of our peace was upon him; and with his stripes we are healed. (Isaiah 53:3-5)

Here is a passage that is often used to convince us that Jesus' death on the Cross was not for our physical healing but that it was referring to emotional and spiritual healing. So let's take a closer look at the words in Hebrew. The passage actually reads: "He was despised and rejected by men, a man of *makob* and familiar with *choli*. ... Surely he took up our *choli* and carried our *makob*."

The word "*makob*" is translated "pain" throughout the Old Testament, and the word "*choli*" is translated "sickness" or "disease." Therefore, the passage actually reads as follows: "He was despised and rejected by men, a man of *pain*, and familiar with *sickness/disease*. ... Surely he took up our *sickness/disease* and carried our *pains*."

Yes, Jesus died for our sins. Yes, He did take our emotional wounds on Himself for us. But He took more to the Cross. We see this underscored in the words of the apostle Matthew, "He ... healed all that were sick: that it might be fulfilled which was spoken by Esaias the prophet, saying, Himself took our infirmities, and bare our sicknesses" (Matthew 8:16-17).

Do you see how Scripture explains itself? Notice that the real meaning of the passage in Isaiah comes through much more accurately and clearly in the translation of the Gospel of Matthew as written in Greek. This is an awesome Scripture, filled with the promise of our healing.

However, do not make the mistake of thinking that it guarantees your wellness any more than the Cross guarantees that you will go to heaven. In order to be saved, you have to reach out and receive Jesus as your Lord and Savior. Likewise, in order to be healed, you have to reach out and receive the healing that was purchased for you by the shed blood of the Cross.

Believe that Jesus did, in fact, take your sicknesses and carry your pains. Walk in the fullness of the victory of the resurrection of Jesus – salvation, deliverance, healing, and being made whole.

Dear God, each day I understand better the full meaning of your Holy Scripture. I thank You for revealing to me the complete sacrifice that Your Son, Jesus Christ, made for me. He bore my sins and my sicknesses and purchased my salvation, freedom, and healing. I rejoice and give thanks. In the mighty name of Jesus, I pray, Amen.

✝

DAY 18
DOES GOD PUT CURSES ON YOU?

But it shall come to pass, if thou wilt not hearken unto the voice of the Lord thy God, to observe to do all his commandments and his statues which I command thee this day; that all these curses shall come upon thee, and overtake thee. ...

The Lord shall smite thee with a consumption, and with a fever, and with an inflammation. ...

The Lord shall smite thee with madness, and blindness, and astonishment of heart.   (Deuteronomy 28:15, 22, 28)

If God never changes, what are we going to do with the lengthy passage in Deuteronomy 28 that lists all the sicknesses that God is going to put on us if we don't observe every single one of His commandments?

God never changes. He is now as He has always been – a God of mercy and also a God of justice. He is both. He gave the people of Israel the law of Moses and told them that there would be consequences if they didn't follow it. The purpose of the law, as Paul explains so well in Romans, was to show people that no matter how hard they tried, they could not keep all the rules, and, therefore, they needed a Savior.

We are the glorious recipients of the life, death, resurrection, and mercy of the Lord Jesus Christ. It is written in Galatians 3:13 that "Christ hath redeemed us from the curse of the law, being made a curse for us." Once and for all, Jesus took all the judgment and all the punishment on Himself that we truly deserve. Matthew 8:17 says that Jesus took all our illnesses on Himself in our place. This means that because God put every disease on Jesus, God won't put them on us. Under the New Covenant, we walk in the grace and mercy of the shed blood of the Cross.

Take a look in Deuteronomy at the list of all the illnesses enumerated there. Look for your health problem. If you find it, speak its name out loud and then say, "That disease is a curse of the law, and Jesus became that curse for me so I don't have to have it."

If you didn't find your illness listed, go to verse 61 which says, "And every sickness, and every plague, which is not written in the book of this law." Isn't God wonderful? He knew there would be some of us who would say that our "modern" disease wasn't listed, so He added a provision that would include every name of every disease whether it was mentioned in the list or not.

So name each ailment that has been attacking you, and after each one say, "That health problem is a curse of the law, and Jesus has redeemed me from the curse of the law." Now lift your voice in praise and thanksgiving. Jesus has borne everything for you – sin and sickness – and has given you salvation, healing, deliverance, and wholeness.

Father God, Jesus became the curse of the disease that is attacking me so that I don't have to bear it myself. He took it, Father. I joyfully proclaim that I walk in the victory won by His shed blood. I am healed because of Jesus! I receive His healing in every cell of my body, and I rejoice and give You thanks. In Jesus' name, I pray, Amen.

SECTION TWO

HINDRANCES THAT COME FROM FOLLOWING THE TRADITIONS OF MEN

Following the traditions of men
can have a devastating effect in your life.
Jesus said that the traditions of men
make the Word of God "of none effect."

✝

DAY 19
MAKING THE WORD OF GOD
OF NONE EFFECT

For laying aside the commandment of God, ye hold the tradition of men, as the washing of pots and cups: and many other such like things ye do. ...

Making the word of God of none effect through your tradition, which ye have delivered: and many such like things do ye. (Mark 7:8, 13)

Jesus makes some very profound statements here as He is talking to the Pharisees and teachers of the law. These are the people in authority, the people who are supposed to have answers, the people who are supposed to know what is the "right" way to do things.

These learned men have criticized Jesus and His disciples for failing to adhere to the "right" way to behave. Specifically, the disciples were seen eating some food without washing their hands first. Jesus tells the Pharisees that they are nullifying the Word of God by holding onto the traditions of men.

Remember this when you feel sick. Family, friends, and health care professionals are quick to try to enforce on you the traditions of men. That is the path that they know and that is the path where they are comfortable. Do not throw out their opinions, but instead, seek the "commands of

God." Go in prayer both with your health advisors and also by yourself to determine what God's path to your healing is. God's path may be the same as the path indicated by men's traditions. On the other hand, it might be some other path that seems foolish or risky to others.

Remember the time that God led the Israelites to a position between the sea and the pursuing Egyptians. Remember the time that God told Noah to build a boat when there had never been anything called "rain." Remember the time that God told Joshua that great walls would tumble down at his shout.

Your healing comes from God and God alone. To make the Word of God of none effect is serious business. God's best is for an instant, complete healing as evidenced by the healings of Jesus. But if it comes gradually over time, its path may be extremely unconventional. God will show you the way, and He will not fail you.

Almighty God, help me to honor Your commands, especially during the times when I feel pressured to follow the traditions of men. I don't want to make Your Words of none effect. When I'm told that I must follow certain medical procedures, I sometimes struggle because I am tempted to allow feelings of fear of making the wrong decision to torment me.

If I follow others and they are wrong, I can say it wasn't my fault. If I do not follow them and something goes wrong, then I will feel foolish and it may be too late to try what they suggest.

Father, make Your guidance known to me so clearly that I am absolutely sure. I will obey You and Your command. And I will stand firm until I receive the manifestation of my healing. In Jesus' name, I pray, Amen.

†

DAY 20
RESULTS OF FOLLOWING
TRADITIONS OF MEN

For ye have heard of my conversation in time past in the Jews'
religion, how that beyond measure I persecuted the church of God,
and wasted it: And profited in the Jews' religion above many my
equals in mine own nation, being more exceedingly zealous of the
traditions of my fathers. But when it pleased God, who separated
me from my mother's womb, and called me by his grace, to reveal
his Son in me, that I might preach him among the heathen;
immediately I conferred not with flesh and blood: Neither went I
up to Jerusalem to them which were apostles before me; but I went
into Arabia, and returned again unto Damascus.
(Galatians 1:13-17)

Paul warns us of the hazards of zealously following the traditions of men, which led him to have many Christians put to death. We, too, must be on guard against slavishly following man's traditions, especially with regard to matters of our health.

Tradition says that God wants certain people to be sick and that He is glorified by their illness. If that is true, then Jesus was constantly interfering with God's glory because He healed every sick person who came to Him.

Think about the number of hospitals, doctors, nurses, and medical treatment facilities we have in this country. If we truly believe that it is God's will for people to be ill and that some divine purpose is worked in their lives by their being sick, then all these facilities and all these people are working contrary to the will of the Lord God Almighty.

It is a strange but common phenomenon of human beings that some people go to church on Sunday and pray that they can accept God's will to bear their illness bravely and then turn around on Monday and race to the doctor to be made well.

Jesus was very clear that every act He did was according to the will of God and that every sick person who came to Him would be healed. One tradition says that these acts of Jesus were miracles only for the people who lived two thousand years ago. But in His last words to us as written in Mark 16:17-18, Jesus said, "and these signs shall follow them that believe; ... they shall lay hands on the sick, and they shall recover." Do you believe Him?

Place your ultimate trust in Father God. Pray with your health care advisors, listen to God's advice, and follow His path for your healing.

Father God, teach me to follow Your way only and to put Your advice before any other. I put aside the traditions of men and stand on Your Word. I trust and believe You. I thank You for healing me, and I ask that You use my life for Your glory and Your service. In Jesus' name, I pray, Amen.

✝

DAY 21
IS IT GOD'S WILL TO HEAL YOU?

And this is the confidence that we have in him, that, if we ask any thing according to his will, he heareth us: and if we know that he hear us, whatsoever we ask, we know that we have the petitions that we desired of him.   (1 John 5:14-15)

John tells us that, if we ask anything according to God's will, He hears us. And if we know that He hears us, we know that we have whatever it is that we asked of Him. Why? Because we have already established that what we are asking is according to His will. It is only when we ask for things outside of God's will that we get into trouble.

It all sounds simple, but, of course, we know from bitter experience that it's not. Satan seeks to get us off the track. He uses our vulnerabilities and weaknesses against us, and he deceives us into believing certain things are God's will when that is, in fact, not true. And he also deceives us into believing other things are not God's will when, in fact, they are. This is the reason that prayer and meditation on God's Word are so important. We have to ask God for His direction in all the small questions of our life as well as the large ones.

You need to get clear in your mind that it is God's will for you to be well. The prayer, "God, please heal me if it's your will" is a doubt-filled prayer that is actually contrary to

93

God's Word. Jesus repeatedly and consistently healed every single person who came to Him to be made whole. It had to be God's will for all to be healed because Jesus healed everyone who came to Him, and He never left anyone sick who received Him.

When you are in harmony with God's will, you know that He has already done what you ask. Therefore, focus on taking action each day according to your guidance. Regardless of the symptoms you may still feel, live with peace in your heart and joy radiating for all to see. Live your life in faith, knowing that nothing is too hard for God and that He has the perfect plan for your highest good.

Declare God's will with confidence and never stop repeating the Scripture on which you are standing in faith. Say constantly to yourself, "Jesus took my infirmities and bore my sicknesses. By the stripes of Jesus I was healed and am healed."

Wonderful Father God, I have confidence in You. It is written that You hear anything I ask that is according to Your will. I know that it is Your will for me to be healed because Your Holy Word says that I was healed by the stripes of Jesus. Thank You, Father, for Your truth. I know You have heard me and I know that I have my healing. Having done all, I will stand until my healing is perfectly manifested. In the mighty name of my Lord Jesus Christ, I pray, Amen.

✝

DAY 22
DO YOU HAVE ANOTHER GOD BESIDES JEHOVAH?

I am the Lord thy God, which have brought thee out of the land of Egypt, out the house of bondage. Thou shalt have no other gods before me. (Exodus 20:2-3)

When people feel sick, most of them turn first to the medical system. They go for a diagnosis, for relief, and for a cure. They usually feel frightened and are often weakened by their illness so that calm thinking is difficult. They are presented with test results and given treatment options. Usually they are told what results to expect. Often they are even told how long they will live if certain things are done or not done.

When confronted with this system of medicine, it is very easy to forget the first and most important commandment: Thou shalt have no other gods before me. What is God saying to us? He is telling us to follow only Him with absolute obedience. He is forbidding us to follow anyone else blindly for any reason. He is telling us to turn to Him and only Him for the answers for our life.

No doctor is God, and his opinion is only that – an opinion. Remember this if you get a chilling diagnosis and prognosis. Do not ignore what he has said because he has told you the best information that he has. But do not accept any doctor's verdict about your condition as divine truth. The knowledge available to him is miniscule compared to the knowledge of the Great I AM.

Only God has provided for your complete healing. He has already done it through the shed blood of the Cross. Only the Great Physician can give you advice and guidance that is pure truth. Go to God. He will meet you where you are and will tell you what is right for you.

Listen to Him and follow His guidance. He loves you with an infinite love. He wants you to be well and will tell you exactly what to do.

Father God, sometimes I struggle to maintain my faith when I hear a doctor tell me that awful things will happen to me and when he holds up my medical tests as proof. I am tempted to succumb to the spirit of fear, but I know that fear does not come from you. I take control over feelings of fear and unbelief and over every thought that is contrary to Your Word, Father God.

I choose to see beyond the appearance of things and refuse to get caught up in symptoms, medical tests, or medical opinions. Reveal to me exactly what you want me to do about my situation. You are divine truth and You do not lie. Your Word tells me that Jesus took my infirmities and bore my sicknesses. Your Word says that by the stripes of Jesus I am healed. I believe You, Father. I believe Your Word. And I receive my healing. In Jesus' name, I pray, Amen.

†
DAY 23
DON'T DIG UP YOUR HARVEST OF HEALING

And he said, So is the kingdom of God, as if a man should cast seed into the ground; and should sleep, and rise night and day, and the seed should spring and grow up, he knoweth not how. For the earth bringeth forth fruit of herself; first the blade, then the ear, after that the full corn in the ear. But when the fruit is brought forth, immediately he putteth in the sickle, because the harvest is come. (Mark 4:26-29)

In His teachings, Jesus used numerous illustrations of a farmer who was planting seeds because that metaphor was perfect to describe the way that God's Word operates and the way that faith matures. God's Word is the living, perfect seed of God's divine truth. "Faith cometh by hearing, and hearing by the word of God," we are told in Romans 10:17. Without the Word of God, there is no faith. We must hear it, receive it, and plant it in our hearts.

Is a planted seed the same thing as a mature plant? Of course not. The seed has the potential to be a mature plant, but it needs time and the proper environment in order to grow, strengthen, and develop. Likewise, the Word of God needs time and the proper environment in order to grow within us.

Too often healing never manifests itself for people because they fail to view their faith in Jehovah-Rapha and in the Word of God as a seed that must be nurtured. They pray for healing and, if they don't see an immediate manifestation, they proclaim that they didn't receive their healing. They are basing their faith on the things they witness with their five senses, even though God's Word is very clear that faith is based on things that are unseen.

What would happen if a farmer dug up his seed every morning to find out if his seed was growing? The answer is so obvious that it is ridiculous. Yet, when we do the same thing with our faith-seeds for health, we think we are being sensible.

Stop judging your healing by analyzing the symptoms that you see. Stand on your faith that God has healed you according to His Word. God paid for your healing two thousand years ago. His healing power was released then. Receive it now and stand until you see it manifest.

Father God, I have planted Your Holy Word in my heart. I join with You in nurturing these seeds as they develop and produce good fruit. I rebuke every effort of the evil one to devour the seed of the Word through lies and deception and to steal Your blessings from me. Give me greater revelation about Your Word, Father, so that I can grow and mature in my understanding. I speak Your Word and declare that You are the God who heals me. Thank You, Father, that my faith-seeds for healing are growing, maturing, and developing and that I will soon see the harvest of healing that I am believing for. In Jesus' name, I pray, Amen.

✝

Day 24
The Biggest Hindrance For Healing Is Your Mouth

Thou art snared with the words of thy mouth, thou art taken with the words of thy mouth. (Proverbs 6:2)

Words are potent – both those spoken and unspoken. What you think and what you say reveal who you really are and provide the spiritual environment in which you exist. If your thoughts and words are positive, healing ones, you are bathing your soul and your body in a soothing stream. If your thoughts and words are negative, doubt-filled ones, you are floundering in a pot of boiling water.

Do you spend a lot of time expressing your doubt that you will be healed? Do you itemize your ailments over and over, emphasizing any increase in symptoms and describing them as further indications of your deterioration? Do you sigh and wish you had faith and then sigh some more?

We build our own prisons with our words. Satan is standing by ready to help us to make the walls thicker and thicker, for he seeks always to trap and deceive us. He loves to convince us that we are "just being honest," and he seeks to confuse us and keep us off balance. He knows that we will sink (or rise) to the level of our words and our thoughts. Every statement or thought that "I'll never be well" or "I'm not getting any better" or "This is as good as I'll ever be" insures that that will indeed be our situation because we are declaring it as our truth.

Abraham acknowledged the "fact" that he and his wife were too old to have a child, yet he learned to look beyond the appearance and speak words of belief and faith in the promise of God. Acknowledge your own "facts." Faith isn't playing pretend. Don't ignore symptoms, "hoping" they will go away. Take authority over them and command them to leave you. If you belong to a church of strong faith-filled and Spirit-filled believers, then have hands laid on you in prayer.

God's best is for you to manifest your healing quickly. But if your healing is manifesting more gradually, hand every element of your health situation over to God in prayer. Make no assumptions about what you should do. Let the Holy Spirit decide what path you should take – whether it be through repentance and spiritual deliverance, through natural healing methods, through medical intervention, or through a combination of them. Follow God's guidance for the perfect solution for you. Voice your belief in God's goodness and speak powerful words of faith and trust.

Almighty God, help me to guard the thoughts that I think and the words that I speak. I choose to fill my mind with Your Word so that I will speak only words of trust, belief, and faith in Your goodness, grace, and power. In Jesus' name, I pray, Amen.

†

DAY 25
WE SPEAK FROM OUR HEART

For a good tree bringeth not forth corrupt fruit; neither doth a corrupt tree bring forth good fruit. For every tree is known by his own fruit. For of thorns men do not gather figs, nor of a bramble bush gather they grapes. A good man out of the good treasure of his heart bringeth forth that which is good; and an evil man out of the evil treasure of his heart bringeth forth that which is evil: for of the abundance of the heart his mouth speaketh. (Luke 6:43-45)

... for out of the abundance of the heart the mouth speaketh. A good man out of the good treasure of the heart bringeth forth good things: and an evil man out of the evil treasure bringeth forth evil things. (Matthew 12:34-35)

The seed contains the potential of the mature plant. What you plant is what you will harvest, if you nurture it to maturity. Jesus describes a truth that is almost ridiculous when viewed in the physical world. If you plant a briar bush, you can't harvest grapes from it. Yet people constantly sow negative seeds with their words by speaking about their ailments and problems and still foolishly expect that they can reap a harvest of healing from it.

Whatever is in our hearts is what will flow out of our mouth in our general conversation. When we say, "My thyroid doesn't work anymore; I'll have to take medication for the rest of my life," we plant a briar bush. Satan wants you to keep speaking his lies as Your truth. He wants you to speak his problems instead of God's solutions.

We have been redeemed from the hand of the enemy. It has already been done. The enemy has no authority over us unless we give it to him. None.

Nevertheless, satan is persistent, and, as the father of lies, he is always ready to take advantage of our weak places. Whenever he can get us to be fearful, he claims a victory. Whenever he can get us to use careless words of death, he claims a victory. Whenever he can get us to stay angry at other people instead of at him, he claims a victory. Whenever he can get us to speak of our symptoms and pains instead of our trust in the flow of God's healing power, he claims a victory.

How can we utter negative words of doom and expect to receive healing? We can't. We have to take control over our mouth and guard every word that comes out of it so that we sow the correct seed that will mature into the outcome we seek.

For example, we can change our words to this: "No matter what the appearance is, no disease can stay in my body. With His stripes I am healed. I call my thyroid whole and healthy. I command it to secrete normal levels of hormones and to be in perfect balance. I enforce the Word on my thyroid, and I thank God for healing me." What a glorious healing "vine" those words plant!

When you feel overwhelmed by the appearance of illness, stand up and say boldly, "I am redeemed by the blood of Jesus Christ, and it is written that I am healed by the stripes He took on His body. Jesus gave me power over all the power of the enemy so I command every lying symptom to leave my body now. Body, I declare that you are healed in the name of Jesus Christ, who bore my infirmities on the Cross. I acknowledge and repent of my sins, and I ask forgiveness. I know that my Redeemer lives, and because He lives, I have life abundantly."

Remember that every word you speak is a seed that determines what kind of result you will have. Immerse yourself in God's Word. Every time you are tempted to speak negative words about your health, quote the Scripture instead. By changing your word-seeds, you will bear good fruit and will be in agreement with God's purpose for your life.

Heavenly Father, let the words of my mouth reflect my full faith in the healing power that You released two thousand years ago through the shed blood of Your Son. Help me to be aware of the times when I sabotage my healing through careless, "faith-less" words. I want to bear good fruit. I know that my mouth speaks out of the overflow of my heart. I want to bring forth good things, so I choose to fill myself with Your Word, which is the true seed and the real treasure. I guard my words and speak my faith. Thank You, Father, for restoring me to wholeness. In Jesus' name, I pray, Amen.

✝

DAY 26
SPEAKING YOUR FEARS

For the thing which I greatly feared is come upon me, and that which I was afraid of is come unto me.   (Job 3:25)

It is a fascinating phenomenon that we draw to ourselves those things to which we give our focus and attention. People who live in a state of fear often find that they have more things about which to be frightened. Life seems to become more and more threatening. The more they become filled with fear, the more they talk about those fears. And with their fear-filled words, they hinder their healing tremendously.

A medical diagnosis of a physical problem generally carries with it a prognosis forecasting the likely result of the disease. Sometimes the prognosis is blindness, being crippled, or even death. Have you received a medical report of similar magnitude? If so, now what do you do?

Your main challenge is to remain grounded in God's Word and to keep your focus on the power of Jehovah-Rapha. God does not send you fear and despair. He sends you strength and healing. A major key is to monitor your thoughts. "Whatsoever things are true, whatsoever things are honest, whatsoever things are just, whatsoever things are pure, whatsoever things are lovely, whatsoever things are of good report; if there be any virtue, and if there be any praise, think on these things" (Philippians 4:8).

Watch the words you speak because you create your world with your words. Pay attention to what you say today. Do you want to live the literal meaning of your words? When you say, "My back is killing me," do you really want to live that experience? When you say, "I'll never be able to walk again," is that what you want? Express your current situation in terms of what you are experiencing for the moment. Be very careful when you use the powerful statement of "I am." Change statements about your health such as "I am tired" to "I feel tired."

Follow the pattern of Christ Jesus who never entertained any fear despite all the obstacles put before Him. He was very clear that with God nothing was impossible. Jesus never forgot His mission which was to deliver God's message of love and to heal God's children.

Determine God's mission for your life and keep your mind focused on it. If fears come to your mind, recognize that many of those thoughts are from satan. Take your authority and renew your mind with the Word. Stay focused on the truth that by His stripes you are healed.

Almighty God, there are times when I have thoughts of fear, but I will not allow them to take root in my mind because they are contrary to the Word of God. I choose to immerse myself in Your Word, Father, and focus on giving You thanksgiving, praise, and glory for the finished work of the Cross. In the mighty name of my Lord Jesus Christ, I pray, Amen.

†

DAY 27
THE DANGER OF MAKING ASSUMPTIONS

Be not wise in thine own eyes: fear the Lord, and depart from evil. It shall be health to thy navel [body], and marrow [strength] to thy bones. (*Proverbs 3:7-8*)

One of the worst traps we can fall into when we have a health problem is to make assumptions about what we should do. We compartmentalize our faith, decide that "things" need to be done, and then just forge ahead and do them.

We think that certain actions are obvious, logical, and "right," so we never think to take them to God in prayer to ask His opinion. When we don't give the power to God, we surely open the door to satan. We are wise in our own eyes and our arrogance often costs us dearly. Sometimes it costs us our lives. And even then, we blame God and moan that it was His will.

The truth is that most of your health problems are a result of numerous poor choices (physical and spiritual) that you have made over a long period of time. When you finally confront the fact that you have a problem, it is time for a complete re-evaluation of the place you have given God in your life.

Consider the matter of prescription drugs. Do you assume all prescriptions are right for you and take them

107

unquestioningly? Make sure you understand each one thoroughly, including the exact beneficial action it is supposed to have in your body and all the undesirable effects (called "side effects") from the package insert provided by the manufacturer of the drug (not the short summary provided by the drug store).

Most people take prescription drugs and know nothing about its precise action in their body. All they know is that it "thins my blood" or something similarly vague. Press for details until you find out, for example, that the prescribed drug stops liver production of certain enzymes. Can you be certain that the drug won't affect other functions of your liver which are essential for a healthy life?

Then, having gathered your information, place the decision for each medication squarely in the hands of the Almighty. He created your body and understands it and its needs better than any human being ever will, including you. He wants you to be well and will instruct you for your highest good.

Ask your doctor to pray with you and to join in partnership with you and God in seeking the best solution for your health problems. The Lord may instruct you to take the medication, or He may not. Just ask Him.

Only God is God. Unless we go to Him first, we will never know what His path for our healing is supposed to be.

Almighty God, I don't want to be wise in my own eyes. I don't want to make assumptions that will hinder or stop my healing. I don't want anyone or anything to be my god above You. You are my God. You are my Lord. You are my healer. You are the only source of truth, Father. Thank You for bringing health to my body and strength to my bones. In the mighty name of Jesus, I pray, Amen.

✝

DAY 28
ARE GERMS THE ENEMY?

O Lord, how manifold are thy works! in wisdom hast thou made them all: the earth is full of thy riches.   (Psalm 104:24)

God made everything that is in the natural world in wisdom. That means that everything has a place in creation and a purpose in creation (even if most of us are still trying to figure out the necessity for the mosquito). Think about the implication of this for a moment. Many bacteria and parasites are vital to the proper functioning of our bodies. God certainly never intended that they kill us.

In the past hundred or so years, the scientific community has developed two predominant theories of health in relation to germs. One viewpoint is the theory expounded by Pasteur which is based on the belief that germs are the cause of disease.

The other viewpoint (held by Claude Bernard and others) is the "law of the terrain," which is based on the belief that toxicity, imbalances in body pH, and other factors are the cause of disease because they create an environment favorable to the growth of germs. Here is an easy-to-understand analogy: flies are attracted to garbage, but they are not the cause of the garbage. Similarly, the terrain theory says that germs are attracted to out-of-balance tissue and thrive there, but they are not the actual cause of the disease.

Today most of us are caught up in the fight to kill all viruses and bacteria we deem as harmful. This external focus on an invading "bug" allows us to take an antibiotic and then to keep on doing just exactly what we want to do in our personal lifestyles. Unfortunately, we find that the germs simply mutate and become more and more resistant to our drugs.

We need to stop playing victim to germs and turn to God for instruction on building a strong terrain within our bodies. We have to accept responsibility for our health and the daily decisions that affect our well-being. Disease cannot live in a body that is functioning in harmony with itself and with the Lord.

God established rules for our good health and knew that, if we are obedient, good health will follow. Turn to the Lord. Ask the Holy Spirit to reveal to you what you need to change in your life so that you can create an environment within that promotes health.

Lord God Almighty, I take responsibility for having made mistakes in taking care of my body. Show me what changes You want me to make, and I will be obedient to follow Your guidance. You have made my temple to be strong and filled with vitality. I thank You for my healing and praise Your Holy name. In Jesus' name, I pray, Amen.

✝

DAY 29
ASK FOR WISDOM

Perseverance must finish its work so that you may be mature and complete, not lacking anything. If any of you lacks wisdom, he should ask God, who gives generously to all without finding fault, and it will be given to him. (James 1:4-5 New International Version)

James, the half-brother of Jesus, speaks of perseverance, maturity, and wisdom. Many people fail to be healed because they lack these essential qualities. We are particularly immature when it comes to matters of our health. We often play the helpless victim to sickness by taking no responsibility for having allowed our bodies to become vulnerable to attacks of the enemy.

We demand one pill or one simple treatment as a cure so that we do not have to make any changes in our lives or confront the spiritual roots of our illness. We say, "I want a quick fix and I'm determined to get it. Just give me a pill to take. What I want is an immediate solution that interferes as little as possible with my life as I choose to live it."

The fact is that man's drugs are actually poisons. Each medicine is tested for its effective dose (ED) and its lethal dose (LD), going to market only when the ED is lower than the LD and being limited to prescription use because of its potential for damage. Even when used according to the

113

directions, the large majority of drugs can cause death. Alarmingly, prescription drugs are now among the top four causes of death in the United States.

Most of man's drugs work by suppressing symptoms and, thus, allow the body relief in order to do its own healing. God's remedies are completely different since their function and purpose are totally opposite. God's "medicine" is actually concentrated food. These herbs and plants do not suppress symptoms but instead nourish, support, and heal the cells and tissue that are not functioning properly.

Herbs are therapeutic in their wholeness when used in the manner and for the purpose that God ordained. We are expected to learn about them and to understand the effect that the Great Physician designed them to have so that we can apply them properly and safely in our recovery program. Isolating and extracting individual components from herbs may be useful; however, that process sometimes carries a significant risk with a negative result.

Healing programs using God's herbs are usually just that - healing programs. You didn't get sick overnight, and there is no pill that is going to correct instantly all the problems you have created. After all, you have most likely spent weeks, months, and often years neglecting and mistreating your body, the temple of the Holy Spirit.

James tells us the blunt truth: if you lack wisdom, ask God. If you want to know what to do about your health, ask the Creator who made your body. God will provide the answers for you, and you must be willing to carry out the instructions He gives.

The Great Physician may lead you to a program combining essential oils, herbs, and natural substances for your recovery, or He may advise you to seek conventional medical treatment. Father God is faithful to meet you where you are in your faith walk, and He is pleased for you to recover in whatever form it takes. Whatever His direction is, God holds you to the test of perseverance and faithfulness to remain steadfast to the course. The Great Physician gives generously and wants you to be well.

Father God, give me wisdom to hear You clearly and perseverance to finish the work You set before me. I choose to follow all of Your instructions because I want to stand under the shield of Your protective covering. You have already provided my healing through the finished work of the Cross, and I give You grateful thanks for the precious sacrifice that was made for me. I will be obedient and will persevere in following all Your guidance, Father, until my body manifests the healing that You have given so generously. In Jesus' name, I pray, Amen.

✝

DAY 30
WE PERISH FOR LACK OF KNOWLEDGE

My people are destroyed for lack of knowledge. (Hosea 4:6)

Information has never before been so voluminous. We are inundated by studies, reports, and new discoveries. There is no one who isn't overwhelmed by it all. It would certainly seem that we have too much knowledge, rather than any lack of it. So is Hosea outdated? Unfortunately, not. This Scripture is still relevant today, especially in the area of recovering our health.

We can look around us and see hundreds and hundreds of herbs and natural substances that are beneficial for our health. Are these just serendipitous results of evolution? No, they are intentional gifts from God, and He expects us to use them.

Ironically, while the majority of the people of the world values these God-given plants, most Americans know almost nothing about them. That is the reason that I continue to emphasize herbs, essential oils, and natural substances. We have convinced ourselves that our own inventions are better than the creations of the Almighty.

Many of us expressed sadness when God was purged from the educational system, and we see evidence that we are reaping what we have sown. Yet no one seems even to notice that God is also purged from our medical system.

One system nourishes minds and the other nourishes bodies. Both need the presence and participation of the Almighty.

There is much to change. Pray that people will learn about God's remedies and will turn to them first when they become ill. Pray that scientists will act in partnership with God, insuring that all experiments and discoveries will be made according to guidance from the Holy Spirit and in harmony with God's purpose for His people.

Pray that doctors will pray with and for their patients so that treatments will not be automatic knee-jerk responses to test results but will be given only on the specific instruction of the Great Physician. Pray that both those seeking to be healed and those gifted with healing abilities will look to the Great Physician for guidance and direction.

Dear Heavenly Father, we have strayed from Your path. And we are dying as a result of it. Help me to do my part to bring You back into our health care system. Guide me to teachers and courses that will show me how to use Your essential oils and herbs for my healing and recovery. I pray now for all doctors, medical personnel, and support people. Help them to place You in the center of their decisions and everything that they do. In the name of Your Son, Jesus Christ, I pray, Amen.

✝

DAY 31
DO NOT BE DRIVEN TO GET RICH

Do not overwork to be rich; because of your own understanding, cease! Will you set your eyes on that which is not? For riches certainly make themselves wings; they fly away like an eagle toward heaven. (Proverbs 23:4-5 New King James Version)

Money is certainly useful and God intends for us to be prosperous. In fact, the Word says that Father God "hath pleasure in the prosperity of his servant" (Psalm 35:27). Our Heavenly Father created a world of great abundance, and we are to enjoy that world. Jesus often used money as illustrations in his parables, and His examples emphasized the importance of multiplication of money as well as its wise and prudent use.

Yet the pursuit of riches as its own goal is a deceptive path. Having money without God is the worst poverty of all. Working day and night for what appears to be the power or security of money depletes you in the end and leaves you with nothing of value. Feeling driven to work has a disastrous effect on your health. The sense of never having enough time and of needing to do more and more in less and less time creates enormous stress in the body that eventually weakens the immune system and many organ systems. This kind of overwork reflects an inner lack of faith in God's timing and God's plan at work in your life.

Take some "time out" to get connected to God. Take an afternoon off or a day off and create a mini-retreat for yourself. Find a place where you can be contemplative and worshipful. If you stay at home, take the phone off the hook and arrange for a private, quiet time alone. Release your concerns to God. Ask Him to set your timetables and to establish your work schedule. Trust Him with your work.

Set aside your tithes, and present your offerings to God as your seed money for His increase and blessing. God's Word says we are to live above the "weak and beggarly elements" (Galatians 4:9) of the world. "Give, and it shall be given unto you; good measure, pressed down, and shaken together, and running over, shall men give into your bosom. For with the same measure that ye mete withal it shall be measured to you again" (Luke 6:38). God wants to bless you with all good things, including prosperity, so that you can be a blessing to others.

Father God, it's easy to get caught up in a struggle for money instead of putting Your principles of increase into operation. I know that it's pure deception to think that having money will solve all of my problems. I trust You and am confident that all my needs be met so that I can be a generous blessing to others. In Jesus' name, I pray, Amen.

✝

Day 32
The Danger Of A Mixture Of Doctrines

Know ye not that to whom ye yield yourselves servants to obey, his servants ye are to whom ye obey; whether of sin unto death, or of obedience unto righteousness?   (Romans 6:16)

The light of the body is the eye: if therefore thine eye be single, thy whole body shall be full of light. But if thine eye be evil, thy whole body shall be full of darkness. If therefore the light that is in thee be darkness, how great is that darkness!   (Matthew 6:22-23)

At the risk of being accused of being judgmental and unloving, I tackle a sensitive subject. If we don't exercise discernment (which is a far different thing from judgment), we will accept every idea from every person out of our love for them. And the result is disastrous. We have to stand for the Word.

We must look at the issue of mixture of doctrines. When we don't have a clear understanding about what was accomplished by the atonement of the Cross, we end up picking and choosing the parts of the Word that we want to believe. The result is a mixture that is only part truth.

Today there seem to be few churches founded on the principle of the Greek word "*soteria*" which is translated "salvation." It is more than just salvation as we use it to mean being saved from our sins. It means "salvation, deliverance, healing, and being made whole." Consequently, most church leaders emphasize only the part of salvation ("*soteria*") which says that Jesus died to atone for our sins. When you attend such a church, you yield yourself to that authority and place yourself in a group of people who do not believe that it is God's will for everyone to be healed.

This can have a very significant impact on your ability to stand for your healing because the doubt and unbelief from others affects you. Remember that Jesus sometimes had to tell people to leave the room when He was praying for their loved ones. Even the Son of God Himself could not do His work in human form where the mixture of belief and unbelief was strong.

Our eye has to remain single (as Jesus tells us in Matthew 6) by staying focused on the complete package of salvation, deliverance, healing, and being made whole without any distraction. Go to the Holy Spirit and seek His counsel to put you in the midst of a group of believers united in their understanding of the fullness of "*soteria*" so that they can stand with you in agreement for your healing.

Father God, my heart is heavy. I have determined not to pick and choose the part of Your Word that I will believe and enforce. I believe that You have provided the complete package through Jesus of salvation, healing, deliverance, and being made whole. Show me the believers you want me to join so that we can join in agreement together for my healing. In Jesus' name, Amen.

SECTION THREE

HINDRANCES THAT COME FROM EMOTIONAL ISSUES

It matters whether you let
your emotions control you
or whether you make a decision
to cultivate joy, peace, and love.

†

DAY 33
FORGIVENESS IS A KEY TO HEALING

Then came Peter to him, and said, Lord, how oft shall my brother sin against me, and I forgive him? till seven times? Jesus saith unto him, I say not unto thee, Until seven times: but, Until seventy times seven.   (Matthew 18:21-22)

A major hindrance to healing is refusal to forgive. Too often people feel justified in carrying their resentment so they take a defiant attitude in refusing to forgive. A surprising number of people do not know what "forgiveness" really means because they confuse it with the concept of pardon.

Forgiveness means to stop carrying resentment against someone who has offended or hurt you. On the other hand, to pardon someone means to excuse him without requiring a penalty for the offense. Do you see the difference?

Forgiveness is really about the person who was hurt and pardoning is more about the person who did the offending. For example, to forgive a spouse who has beaten you does not mean that you have to continue to live with that abuse. To forgive someone who raped you does not mean that that person should not go to prison for his actions.

Jesus tells you to forgive so many times that you lose count in the process. Why? Because unforgiveness is really

125

sin and provides an open door to the enemy. Resentment takes a heavy toll on your physical and spiritual health. Resentment does not hurt the person who offended you at all. It is not affecting him, but it is killing you. Like all sin, it destroys your soul, saps your energy, and gives the devil control in your life.

By holding onto resentment, you become an offender against yourself. You recreate the offense over and over again and re-wound yourself. The new offender is you, yourself, and not the other person.

Are you carrying hurts or anger toward someone? Resentment is a powerful negative emotion that colors everything we do. It triggers responses in us when situations come up that don't even involve the offender.

It creates a great deal of stress not only on our emotions but also on our bodies. Often illness and even injuries from accidents result from resentment and its resulting anger which we nurture inside. Our refusal to forgive and to let go of our resentment carries a heavy price indeed.

You cannot heal when you are filled with the spirit of resentment toward anyone, whether it is someone else or whether it is your own self. You must reach the point where you are willing to forgive others and, just as important, to forgive yourself of all things you regret doing or not doing. Let the past go. Get delivered from all anger, resentment, and hurt, and then allow God's healing power to flow through you.

Heavenly Father, I have been carrying some old hurts inside for a long time. I know now that I have been the one hurting myself by harboring the spirit of resentment. Thank You, Father, for forgiving me, as I now choose to forgive those who have hurt me. I also forgive myself for carrying this unforgiveness all these years. I take every offense, every hurt, and every resentment and erase them now. I choose to walk forward in the lightness of freedom and deliverance. In Jesus' name, I pray, Amen.

✝

DAY 34
HOW DO YOU FORGIVE?

And forgive us our sins; for we also forgive every one that is indebted to us. (Luke 11:4)

And when ye stand praying, forgive, if ye have ought against any: that your Father also which is in heaven may forgive you your trespasses. But if ye do not forgive, neither will your Father which is in heaven forgive your trespasses. (Mark 11:25-26)

Jesus repeatedly taught on forgiveness because He knew that there is no freedom without it. The bondage of the spirits of unforgiveness, resentment, and anger is crippling to our souls and damaging to our bodies.

So how do you forgive? Begin by writing down the name of every person who has ever hurt you, even those you think you have already forgiven. Sometimes we think we have forgiven someone, yet what we have really done is to bury our feelings so deep inside ourselves that we do not consciously feel the hurt anymore. Take plenty of time in making your list so you can be thorough.

When you are ready, say each name on the list and then tell that person that you forgive him or her. Forgive yourself for carrying the resentment all this time. Then repent to God and ask His forgiveness.

Next, ask the Holy Spirit for advice on the appropriate way to ask forgiveness and to make amends directly to each person. Some people on your list may not be living. For those who are living, you may choose to write a letter, make a phone call, or visit them in person. In some cases, the Holy Spirit may tell you not to make direct contact when there were issues such as abuse.

Tearing up your list or burning it can serve as a symbol of your letting go. If you become aware of feelings of resentment sneaking back in, take immediate authority over those thoughts and feelings. Do not allow the enemy to bring you into bondage again.

Once you have forgiven all those who have hurt you, you will experience a wonderful release. You have been imprisoned by the past and now walk freely in the present. Rejoice in the peace and calmness that comes from forgiving and being forgiven.

Dear Father, I have forgiven all those who have hurt me. I take authority over every thought and emotion of unforgiveness, resentment, anger, and victimization, and I renew my mind daily by meditating on Your Holy Word. Thank You, Father, for forgiving me, cleansing me, freeing me, and healing me. In Jesus' name, I pray, Amen.

✝

DAY 35
MAKE RESTITUTION

And Jesus entered and passed thorough Jericho. And, behold, there was a man named Zacchaeus, which was the chief among the publicans, and he was rich. And he sought to see Jesus who he was; and could not for the press, because he was little of stature. And he ran before, and climbed up into a sycamore tree to see him: for he was to pass that way. And when Jesus came to the place, he looked up, and saw him, and said unto him, Zacchaeus, make haste, and come down; for today I must abide at thy house.

And he made haste, and came down, and received him joyfully. And when they saw it, they all murmured, saying, That he was gone to be a guest with a man that is a sinner.

And Zacchaeus stood, and said unto the Lord; Behold, Lord, the half of my goods I give to the poor; and if I have taken any thing from any man by false accusation, I restore him fourfold.

And Jesus said unto him, This day is salvation come to this house, forsomuch as he also is a son of Abraham. For the Son of man is come to seek and to save that which was lost. (Luke 19:1-10)

Zacchaeus teaches us an important lesson about repentance and about making restitution. Because of his actions, Jesus said to him, "This day is salvation come to this house, forsomuch as he also is a son of Abraham. For the Son of man is come to seek and to save that which was lost."

We are a whole unit – spirit, soul, mind, emotions, and body. When we have violated someone and have not made restitution, we are damaged spiritually and we are also damaged mentally and emotionally. If we allow our transgression to fester long enough, it may also create physical damage as well. Why? Because we have become vulnerable to the evil one. This is a chink in the armor described in Ephesians 6, and his arrow can get through and pierce us.

To be made whole, we have to get right with God and with our fellow man. Own up to your mistakes and, like Zacchaeus, make restitution where it is possible or appropriate to do so. Ask the Holy Spirit for guidance for each particular situation and act according to the instructions that you are given.

You cannot be made whole if you are carrying burdens of guilt and ill will. Be willing to atone for your wrongdoings and allow the Lord's peace to fill your soul.

Father God, help me to examine my life honestly and to make a list of wrongs I've committed against others. I choose to atone for my mistakes and make the best restitution that I can. Where it is no longer possible or wise to do so directly to the people I have wronged, show me what You would have me do. I need healing for my soul as well as my body. Thank You, Father, for Your salvation, deliverance, and healing. In Jesus' name, I pray, Amen.

✝

Day 36
Get Things Right With Your Brother

Moreover if thy brother shall trespass against thee, go and tell him his fault between thee and him alone: if he shall hear thee, thou hast gained thy brother. But if he will not hear thee, then take with thee one or two more, that in the mouth of two or three witnesses every word may be established. And if he shall neglect to hear them, tell it unto the church: but if he neglect to hear the church, let him be unto thee as an heathen man and a publican.
(Matthew 18:15-17)

Your physical health is integrally connected to your emotional and spiritual health. If you are carrying sorrow, grief, anger, or bitterness toward a family member or friend or acquaintance, whether living or dead, that inner pain is affecting your health in a negative way. You cannot carry negative feelings without paying a price.

Jesus gives us an important lesson here in how to handle the situation. In this particular passage Jesus refers to a situation in which your brother (actually a broad term including any believer) has wronged you, and He shows us how to do what we can to work things out. Go to your brother and try to work things out. If that is not successful, go to him again with a couple of other believers. If that is not successful, ask your pastor for assistance. If none of those methods bring reconciliation, then you have done everything you can do.

Notice that you must be heard, but you are to be persistent in trying to work things out only up to a point. You are not supposed to keep trying to force things to be amenable because in doing so you violate both yourself and the other person. Remember that God forces no one to love Him; you must allow others the same freedom – the right not to love you. Also remember that Jesus said that His family was those who followed Him and acted according to God's will, not simply those into whose family He was born.

Ask God for the courage to move on with your life. Perhaps someday they will accept you, but in the meantime do not continue to mourn the past or to try to force certain relationships. Pray for them earnestly and trust God to bring new family into your life. You will experience a new freedom, and you will find healing not only for your soul but also your body.

Loving Father, I have been to my brother, asked forgiveness for my part in the trouble between us, and I have not been received. I forgive him, Father, and release every resentment and hurt that I have been holding. Give me courage to let go in love and to stop replaying the relationship I have missed. Hold my brother in Your loving arms, Father, and help Him to find Your truth and peace. Help me to develop strong relationships with the people you want me to have as family and friends. In Jesus' name, I pray, Amen.

✝

DAY 37
STOP BEING CRITICAL

And why beholdest thou the mote that is in thy brother's eye, but perceivest not the beam that is in thine own eye?

Either how canst thou say to thy brother, Brother, let me pull out the mote that is in thine eye, when thou thyself beholdest not the beam that is in thine own eye? Thou hypocrite, cast out first the beam out of thine own eye, and then shalt thou see clearly to pull out the mote that is in thy brother's eye.   (Luke 6:41-42)

If you focus on the faults of others, you are creating an unfavorable environment in your mind and your body. Being critical and negative is not only a major hindrance to healing but also one of the roots of illness and disease. A constant fault-finding attitude often characterizes a person who is unforgiving.   Creating more than spiritual and emotional wounds, resentment also leads to physical imbalances within the body.

Negativity actually upsets your immune system by depleting your energy and draining vitality from your cells. It was no accident that Jesus, our perfect Healer, consistently taught the importance of forgiveness and of approaching life with a positive, loving heart.

As an experiment, carry a little notebook around for a few days. Each time you make a remark that is critical of some person, event, or thing, jot it down, along with the time. At the end of the day, take a look at your list. Is there any pattern that is apparent? Are there particular times of day when you were more negative? For example, were you more negative when you were involved in certain activities, such as driving or doing certain chores or being with particular people?

Decide whether you want to end these habits of negative criticism. If so, take responsibility for your thought life and cancel every negative thought that comes to your mind. If you stay in an overwhelming struggle, consider deliverance to bring the relief and release that Jesus bought for you on the cross.

Each time that you find yourself becoming stressed and critical, take a deep breath, say a prayer to release your irritation, and allow God's love and joy to fill your mind and every cell in your body. Say "thank you" to God for transforming, changing, and redeeming you.

Almighty God, I take responsibility for my thought life, and I cancel every negative thought that comes to my mind. I'm going to work harder at dealing with my own issues instead of finding fault in everyone else. Starting today, I choose to release resentment and bitterness, and instead I will look with eyes of compassion on my friends, family, and others. In Jesus' name, I pray, Amen.

✝

DAY 38
HOW DO YOU SHOW LOVE?

Ye are my friends, if ye do whatsoever I command you. Henceforth I call you not servants; for the servant knoweth not what his lord doeth: but I have called you friends; for all things that I have heard of my Father I have made known unto you. Ye have not chosen me, but I have chosen you, and ordained you, that ye should go and bring forth fruit, and that your fruit should remain: that whatsoever ye shall ask of the Father in my name, he may give it you. These things I command you, that ye love one another. (John 15:14-17)

Repeatedly, Jesus exhorts and encourages every believer to follow through with His instructions. Notice that in this verse His instruction is a commandment, not a suggestion or an idea for us to consider. Jesus tells us that what He is saying is part of the "musts" of life. You must do what I am telling you if you want the result I promise, He declares. You have to do it this way. There are definite strings to the gift that is offered.

What is the command? To love. We know we feel love for certain people. But love as a feeling is weak because love is really action. It comes to life in what we do. And Jesus sets the standard very high by telling us we are to love everyone including our enemies.

Take some time to make an accounting of the ways that you act your love. Set aside a few minutes at the end of the day to list five ways that you put your love in action during the day. Maybe you prepared dinner for your family with a song in your heart and love flowing into the food instead of with complaints and pressure and unhappiness. Maybe you wrote a "thinking of you" card that you had put off for days. Maybe you spent some extra time brushing your pet and giving him attention.

If we want to fulfill our purpose, we have to get in the love business. Remember the incident when at the age of 12 Jesus had gotten separated from His earthly parents in Jerusalem and was found teaching in the synagogue? He told Mary and Joseph that He had to be about His Father's business.

Here He tells us that we are now in the Father's love business. If we fail to let the love of God flow through us to others, then we put up a major block to our healing because healing from the Lord rides on His love. Jesus has chosen us, and He has told us everything we need to know. It is up to us to respond to the call.

Gracious Father, thank You for the love You shower on me every minute of every day. I want to be about Your business of spreading Your Word and of being a living example of Your love to all who see me. Let me be a glorious example for others, manifesting my healing to Your glory. In the name of Your Son, Jesus Christ, Amen.

✝

DAY 39
LOVE GOD

But as it is written, Eye hath not seen, nor ear heard, neither have entered into the heart of man, the things which God hath prepared for them that love him. (1 Corinthians 2:9)

In your wildest imagination you can't picture all the wondrous things which your Heavenly Father wants to give you. One of the blessings that God wants His children to have is good health. When He created the Garden of Eden, He provided that Adam and Eve should be healthy, strong, and vital. There was no sickness or disease that could harm them.

Jesus came to show God's will for us, doing only those things that were according to God's plan and purpose. He healed everyone who came to Him to be made well. And when our time on this earth is done, we know that we will go to heaven, where God's perfect will always reigns. In the place of God's abode, there is no sickness or disease.

There is one requirement: that we love and obey God. Love is not simply an emotion that we feel. It consists of hundreds of thousands of actions minute by minute, based on our decisions and intent. Love is what you do. To love God means that you trust God with your entire being. To love God means that you ask Him for guidance in your life.

To love God means that you obey the instructions that you are given.

Most Christians think that they love, trust, and obey God at least most of the time. However, when they feel sick, the pattern is often to follow conventional methods of dealing with illness automatically. As long as the treatments are working or are not life-threatening, people rarely involve God in their recovery. It is only when surgery is pending or the treatments aren't working, that many go to God in prayer.

God does not want to be an afterthought. He wants to be your first consultation. To love God is to trust Him with your life and to be willing to seek His advice first. To love God is to be willing to obey His directives for your healing, regardless of what they might be. Stand fast in your love for Him. Stand fast in your trust that your eye has not seen and your ear has not heard nor has it entered into your heart the things which God has prepared for you.

Father God, it is written that eye hath not seen nor ear heard, neither have entered into the heart of man, the things which You have prepared for those who love You. I love You, Lord. I love You. I believe Your Word and I trust You. I act on my faith, seek Your advice, and obey Your voice. Thank You, Father, for saving me, healing me, delivering me, prospering me, and making me whole. In the name of Your Son, Jesus Christ, I pray, Amen.

✝

DAY 40
LOVE AND HEALING WORK TOGETHER

Nay, in all these things we are more than conquerors through him that loved us.

For I am persuaded, that neither death, nor life, nor angels, nor principalities, nor powers, nor things present, nor things to come, nor height, nor depth, nor any other creature, shall be able to separate us from the love of God, which is in Christ Jesus our Lord. (Romans 8:37-39)

God is love. God loves you more than you can possibly comprehend. Can you take this truth into the very core of your being? Can you absorb it fully? Love is holy because it is the essence of God. Yet sadly, it is often elusive to many people.

We think of love as an emotion, as something we feel. Yet it is much more than a feeling. Love is defined and expressed much more by action than by feelings. It is far easier to say "I love you" than it is to live "I love you." And therein lies the key to the reason that many people don't trust love. They have been betrayed once too often by people who claimed to love them. So they withdraw inside and put up a protective wall to shield themselves.

Illness often follows because we need love like flowers need water. Our health depends on the constant flow of giving and receiving love, like a great circle of divine smiles. Love is holy, healing, and connecting.

Look deep within your heart. Do you allow God's love to flow freely to you? Or do you feel unworthy? Do you remember times from long ago when you felt alone and abandoned, and do you still carry those feelings? Do you fear being betrayed?

These emotions are all blocks to God's love. In order to be well physically, you will need to face these inner conflicts, to let them go, and to be delivered from them.

Hear Paul tell you that nothing, absolutely nothing, can stand in the way of God's love for you. God loves you so much that He sent His Son to redeem you completely. He sent His Son to forgive your sins and to heal your body. He sent His Son for you.

Father God, thank You for Your great love for me. I allow myself to be open to Your love so that it can flow through every part of my being. There is no power that can separate me from Your awesome love, and I rejoice in knowing that I am never, ever alone and unloved. You are always with me, loving me, encouraging me, and protecting me. I feel tears of joy as I allow Your love to heal my soul, my mind, my emotions, and my body. In Jesus' name, I pray, Amen.

✝

Day 41
There Is No Fear In Love

There is no fear in love; but perfect love casteth out fear: because fear hath torment. He that feareth is not made perfect in love. (1 John 4:18)

There is no fear in love. When we absorb God's love into the depths of our being, we will be at peace. We all seem to strive for this, but few seem to attain it. Why is this so?

Fear is one of the primary tools of satan. In fact, fear is one of the devil's primary powers and principalities. The enemy takes every opportunity to remind us of our fears and tries to keep us focused on them. Eventually, he often even gets us to learn to love our fears or become addicted to them. Being fearful allows us to seek reassurance from our family and friends over and over again.

When we feel sick, our symptoms can change every day or every week, providing ample opportunity for giving us something new to be fearful about. Fear tries to suck us in, and it keeps us just where satan wants us. We are no longer focused on God's Word. We are no longer sure of God's will. And we are no longer certain that the finished work of the Cross includes our healing.

However, to live in fear is a choice and to live in love is a choice. God allows us the free will to decide whether to choose love over fear. He extends His love to us every minute of every day and wants us to have it. His love is so boundless that He sent His Son for our salvation and healing.

Each time you feel fear about your health, replace it with a faith-seed from the Word of God. Quickly take captive every thought of fear, and renew your mind with victorious proclamations of Scripture.

Speak the Word, modifying Scripture to make it personally applicable to you. "I am the Lord that heals you" (Exodus 15:26). "By His stripes I was healed" (1 Peter 2:24). "Jesus Christ Himself took my infirmities and bare my sicknesses" (Matthew 8:17). "If I have faith as a grain of mustard seed, I shall say unto this mountain, 'Remove hence to yonder place,' and it shall remove; and nothing shall be impossible unto me" (Matthew 17:20). "He sent His Word and healed me" (Psalm 107:20).

Over and over again, speak the Word. Enforce it on every cell, tissue, gland, and organ of your body. Trust, believe, and accept God's love and healing with grateful thanks.

Dear Heavenly Father, thank You for surrounding and enfolding me in the perfect safety of Your love. I break the bondage of fear and take every thought of worry and anxiety captive. I choose You, Your love, and Your healing. I choose to be well. In Jesus' name, I pray, Amen.

✝

DAY 42
GOD HAS NOT GIVEN US
A SPIRIT OF FEAR

For God hath not given us the spirit of fear; but of power, and of love, and of a sound mind. (2 Timothy 1:7)

God does not want us to be fearful. Repeatedly, He proclaims in His Word, "Fear not." Jesus' birth was heralded with the glorious announcement, "Fear not: for, behold, I bring you good tidings of great joy!" (Luke 2:10). Paul delivers the same message to us again in 2 Timothy.

Fear is the tool of the evil one. It keeps us victimized by illness and by people's actions, and it makes us weak. Fear separates us from God and keeps us from accepting God's true gifts.

What does God give us? Power! Not power over people to control them, but power to transform ourselves. Power to fulfill God's purpose in our lives. Power to spread God's Word to others. Power to overcome obstacles in our path. Jesus told us He brought us power ("*dunamis*") over all the power of the enemy, including sickness and disease.

God also gives us love which is the core of our Heavenly Father's essence. Jesus kept telling us, "God loves you! Love God and worship Him. As God loves you, love others. And as God loves you, love yourself. Love your neighbor as yourself."

When we connect to God's love and allow it to flow within our souls and bodies, we are healed. Love is the most powerful force in existence. It is infinitely stronger than sickness.

Lastly, God gives us a sound mind, also translated as "self-control" or "self-discipline." These are our tools to do what we need to do. God always requires that we take action. We have to make the decisions to eat foods that are healthy for us, to get enough rest, to make time to play and laugh, and to walk, dance, or exercise.

All of this takes self-control and self-discipline. It is up to us to be willing to resist the temptations of the evil one and to align ourselves with God by following His guidelines for healthy living.

Father God, thank You for giving me power, love, self-discipline, self-control, and a sound mind. I accept these gifts to help me fulfill Your purpose for my life. I take authority over the spirit of fear, and I renew my mind by meditating on Your Holy Word. I choose to exercise self-control by doing those things which I know are healthy and avoiding those things which contribute to my illness. I speak to my body, and I command every cell to function perfectly according to Your divine plan. Thank You, Father, for loving me and holding me in Your protective arms. In the name of Your Son, Jesus Christ, I pray, Amen.

†

Day 43
Trade Fear For Peace

Peace I leave with you, my peace I give unto you: not as the world giveth, give I unto you. Let not your heart be troubled, neither let it be afraid. (John 14:27)

How often the message of God's Word tells us not to be afraid. Fear does not come from God. Fear is the work of the devil, and it separates us from God because love and fear cannot operate simultaneously.

God is perfect love. Jesus, as part of the Holy Trinity of Father, Son, and Holy Spirit, is also perfect love. In Him there was and is no room for fear. Whether confronted with satan, bad weather, multitudes of needy people, or a betrayer's kiss, Jesus remained at peace, centered in total love and peace.

Jesus calls you to Him and asks you to trust Him. "I give you my peace," He said. "Don't be afraid." The devil knows all our weaknesses, and he sends thoughts of fear to drive and torment us, including fears of being lonely, unloved, unworthy, poor, abused, rejected, and abandoned.

Deep in our heart, a surprising number of us are afraid of being healthy. If we feel sick, we have an excuse to fail. If we feel sick, we have a reason to protect ourselves from a dangerous world. If we feel sick, we have "permission" to ask for kindness from others. As long as we receive these hidden benefits from illness, our fears of being well are triggered, and the true desire of our heart is really to be sick. We must first cast the enemy and every spirit of fear out of us in order to create the proper environment for our healing.

Choosing to live in faith instead of in fear would seem to be an easy choice, but it isn't. Jesus knows it takes courage to let go of our fears. He tells us He will help us and that He has His precious peace to give us.

We have to renew our minds and shift our focus. Confess the Word of God on a daily basis, and, if the fears try to return, take charge of your thoughts and banish the fears immediately. Accept the peace of Christ in your heart and nestle under the wings of Jehovah-Rapha.

Almighty God, I am sorry for the times I have allowed fear to take root. I now choose to renew my mind with Your Holy Word and replace every fear with faith and love. I won't let my heart be burdened with troubles, but I'll cast them on Jesus as He told me to do. Thank You for enfolding me in Your loving, protective arms and surrounding me with Your strength, Your healing power, and the peace of Your Son, Jesus Christ, my Redeemer. I worship You, Father, and I bless Your Holy name. In Jesus' name, I pray, Amen.

✝

Day 44
Do You Love Yourself?

... Thou shalt love thy neighbour as thyself. (Matthew 19:19)

Most Christians hear only the "love your neighbor" portion of these words of Jesus. They ignore the "as yourself" phrase because they are fearful of being accused of being selfish and self-centered. Consequently, Christians often have a great deal of trouble following this commandment.

Our failure to do so is one reason that we frequently fall into ill health. We get caught up in taking care of others and neglect to take care of ourselves with equal concern and diligence. Never forget that your body is the temple of the Holy Spirit. Helping others is a major way that we serve God, but if we do so without giving equal regard to our own temples, we violate God's will and plan for us.

The enemy often wants us to feel guilty no matter what we do. If we consider our own needs, he tries to condemn us with accusations of selfishness. Yet if we overwork by doing for others, he tries to condemn us with guilty feelings that we deserve sickness because we didn't take care of ourselves properly. Take authority over all these thoughts from the enemy and renew your mind with God's truth.

Notice that Jesus didn't say to love your neighbor either more or less than yourself – but equal to yourself. Jesus is telling you that you must be self-full rather than self-ish. This means allowing God's love to fill you so that you take care of yourself lovingly, just as you take care of others.

Think about the little kindnesses you do for your family, friends, and neighbors. List specific examples of ways that you help them. Now ask yourself when you applied those same kindnesses to yourself. Take a few minutes to reflect on how this has impacted your health. What priority do you give to living healthily and taking care of your own body? Decide what you need to do to make a change so that you can join in partnership with God to support your body in recovery.

Since we live in a frantic world and our lives are filled to the brim with activities, we must refocus on God's will for us. Jesus tells us that God wants us to serve Him by loving our neighbors and ourselves equally. Treat your body with the same kindness, respect, and care that you give to others.

Almighty God, too often I don't follow this commandment that Your Son gave to me. I get caught up in my busy life, and I never seem to have enough time to do what I ought to be doing. Help me, Father, to learn to take the time to care for myself in a loving, nurturing way and most of all to take time to deepen my relationship with You through worship, prayer, and reading Your Word. In Jesus' name, I pray, Amen.

✝

DAY 45
GET RID OF EMOTIONAL BAGGAGE

There is a time for everything and a season for every activity under heaven: a time to be born and a time to die, a time to plant and a time to uproot, a time to kill and a time to heal, a time to tear down and a time to build, a time to weep and a time to laugh, a time to mourn and a time to dance, a time to scatter stones and a time to gather them, a time to embrace and a time to refrain, a time to search and a time to give up, a time to keep and a time to throw away, a time to tear and a time to mend, a time to be silent and a time to speak, a time to love and a time to hate, a time for war and a time for peace. (Ecclesiastes 3:1-8 New International Version)

Often the emotional baggage that you carry makes you sick. You must be willing to deal with these issues if you really want to be well. Unless you are willing to look within at your emotions, your motivations, and your desires, you are not likely to recover in your physical body.

Your emotions and your body interrelate, each affecting the other and each being affected by the other. Healing does not happen when you continue behaving in ways that made you sick in the first place.

It is necessary to examine yourself and to perform some internal housecleaning. The Scripture in Ecclesiastes says that there is a time to search and a time to give up. So what will you keep and what will you throw away?

Are you willing to expose your guilt, shame, and hurts – and then be released from them? Make no mistake about it; to leave a wound inside is to leave a festering pocket of poison that has probably affected your physical body and contributed to your illness. Many people are very adept at stuffing these wounds so deeply that they convince themselves that they have gotten rid of them. Yet the real truth is that the emotional poison seeps out and eventually creates a physical problem that can sometimes become deadly.

If you have been standing for your healing and have not seen it manifest, one possible reason is that you are being hindered by these negative emotions. This is the time to get rid of them and walk in freedom. Are you willing? Experience the freedom that Jesus won for you on the Cross.

Almighty God, I admit that I have been carrying negative emotional baggage for a long time. I really haven't thought that there was any relationship between my health problems and my hurt and disappointment and grief and anger. But now I see that it is time to search for these negative emotions and let them go. Thank You for helping me to uproot everything that is ungodly so that I may dance in the joy of Your freedom. In the name of Christ Jesus, my Savior and my Redeemer, I pray, Amen.

✝

Day 46
Stop Worrying

Casting the whole of your care [all your anxieties, all your worries, all your concerns, once and for all] on Him, for He cares for you affectionately and cares about you watchfully. (1 Peter 5:7 Amplified Bible)

If you ask a rational person if he would rather be loaded down with worries or if he would rather be literally "care-free," he would undoubtedly tell you that he would prefer to have no burdens. We know that Jesus specifically told us to give Him our burdens. In fact, we know that Jesus has already carried our heaviest burdens to the Cross. He has already atoned for our sins, and He has already borne our sicknesses. It has already been done.

Yet here almost all of us are, steeped in worry, especially when we feel sick. How worry consumes us! It saps our energy, depletes our emotional and physical reserves, and yet most people still do it! Jesus stands before us, ready and willing for us to hand our concerns to Him. It ought to be the easiest thing in the world to do. It is certainly easy to say the words, "Jesus, I give my worries and my cares to you." But the words are empty without actions to bring them meaning.

To live those words, you must believe that God is all-loving and that He wants you to be well. You must believe that God is all-powerful and that nothing is impossible to those who believe in Jehovah-Rapha. You must believe that your healing was won on the Cross and that God's healing power is flowing in a constant stream toward you. All you have to do is to receive it.

More often than not, you may find yourself tempted to pick back up the worries you have given to the Lord. When that happens, don't beat yourself up. Keep developing your spiritual strength, so that you can take charge of your thoughts and renew your mind. Turn your cares over to God one more time. God understands and He cares for you watchfully.

Father God, sometimes I allow myself to be deceived by the enemy and let myself be overwhelmed with worry. It seems that there are so many decisions to make that I am tempted to feel discouraged and fearful. Father, the truth is that there are days when it would seem easier to crawl in bed, pull the covers over my head, and hide. But I am not going to give in to those feelings because You have told me to take responsibility and not play the role of a victim.

In the name of Jesus, I take charge of my thoughts, and I do as Peter exhorts me and cast all my cares and worries and concerns on You. I praise You, Father, and glorify Your name. In the name of Your Son, Christ Jesus, my Savior and my Redeemer, I pray, Amen.

†

DAY 47
DON'T BE CHOKED BY THE CARES
OF THIS WORLD

He also that received seed among the thorns is he that heareth the word; and the care of this world, and the deceitfulness of riches, choke the word, and he becometh unfruitful.   (Matthew 13:22)

And these are they which are sown among thorns; such as hear the word, and the cares of this world, and the deceitfulness of riches, and the lusts of other things entering in, choke the word, and it becometh unfruitful.   (Mark 4:18-19)

And that which fell among thorns are they, which, when they have heard, go forth, and are choked with cares and riches and pleasures of this life, and bring no fruit to perfection.   (Luke 8:14)

Jesus tells us that, if we take on the cares of this world, we will become unfruitful. This is a strong Word from the Lord about the danger of failing to turn over every burden to Him.

How often do you find yourself feeling overwhelmed and frustrated? If your car breaks down for the second time in a month, what is your immediate response? Frustration and despair?

If you are rushing to finish a project and your computer suddenly doesn't function properly, what is your immediate reaction? Anger and panic?

If you look at your bank balance and the bills have eaten up your money faster than it's being replenished, what is your immediate response? Depression and defeat?

It is easy to be spiritual when everything is going well. The real tests come when challenges arrive. Those are the times that you find out if the Word is really working in you. Do you turn to God first? Or do you try to figure a solution out all on your own?

Jesus said to give your burdens to Him. Through Him we have the victory over everything that happens to us. If we stay focused on Him, He will guide us through every difficulty and every care of this world. That trust enforces the Word and results in your bearing much fruit. Turn your cares over to the Lord and rest in Him.

Father God, I'm tired of letting myself be choked by the cares of this world. You have told me to give every burden to You, but I too often hold onto them. Today I set myself with a new resolve to stand against overwhelming situations that come my way and to turn every frustration over to You. I don't want to let Your precious Word become of none effect in my life because I keep trying to handle everything on my own. I want to be fruitful, Father. In Jesus' name, I pray, Amen.

†

DAY 48
ATTITUDES THAT DESTROY

These six things doth the Lord hate: yea, seven are an abomination unto him: a proud look, a lying tongue, and hands that shed innocent blood, an heart that deviseth wicked imaginations, feet that be swift in running to mischief, a false witness that speaketh lies, and he that soweth discord among brethren.
(Proverbs 6:16-19)

Keeping yourself mentally and spiritually grounded is vital to your physical good health. As soon as you become vulnerable to the evil one, your body is open for illness and disease to take hold.

What things make us particularly vulnerable? Of course, there are many, but these verses in Proverbs list several. Pride, lying, killing innocent people, evil actions, causing dissension, lying, and sowing discord. Isn't it interesting that lying and causing discord appear twice? When you get off track internally, you have moved from being in agreement with God to being in agreement with satan. People who engage in these activities are being manipulated by the enemy.

How do the items listed relate to your health problems? They are often the source of them because they are all satan's seeds. If they find fertile soil within you, then they can grow into illness. Once you have a health problem, if you continue to cultivate these qualities, you will have a very hard time getting well.

Pride and arrogance in particular lock you into illness because they lead you to assume you know what actions you should take. These assumptions are often wrong, yet you are so sure they are right that you never ask God what His opinion is. Before you take action, pray and ask for guidance.

Sometimes people find they are routinely and habitually engaging in these activities and they just can't stop. When this is the case, it usually indicates that there are deliverance issues involved.

The really good news is that the Word says that Jesus "spoiled powers and principalities" (Colossians 2:15). Some of these demonic principalities are the very ones we are talking about – pride, lying, murder, and strife. But Jesus has "made a show of them openly, triumphing over them" (Colossians 2:15) so you can walk in the freedom He has won for you.

Father God, sometimes I can't seem to stop myself from doing things that I know are wrong. I know my spirit is pure before You, but my soul still struggles. I know that You have provided every benefit for me – salvation, healing, deliverance, and being made completely whole. Show me Your truth, Father, and Your path for me. In the name of Your Son, Jesus Christ, I pray, Amen.

✝

DAY 49
THE DAMAGING EFFECTS OF STRIFE

For where envying and strife is, there is confusion and every evil work. (James 3:16)

He that is of a proud heart stirreth up strife: but he that putteth his trust in the Lord shall be made fat. (Proverbs 28:25)

An angry man stirreth up strife, and a furious man aboundeth in transgression. (Proverbs 29:22)

Cast out the scorner, and contention shall go out; yea, strife and reproach shall cease. (Proverbs 22:10)

Where no wood is, there the fire goeth out: so where there is no talebearer, the strife ceaseth. (Proverbs 26:20)

He loveth transgression that loveth strife: and he that exalteth his gate seeketh destruction. (Proverbs 17:19)

Look at all these warnings about strife. What is strife? It is conflict, struggle, discord. And it is one of the most powerful tools in the enemy's arsenal. If satan can get people in conflict with each other, then he has an environment to stir up every evil work.

The Word of God gives us many warnings about potential sources of strife. Pride. Anger. Contempt. Scorn. Gossip. Sinful behavior. Emotions fester and then burst out to rupture our relationships with other people and even with God. Our hurts then drive us to make more

159

unwise choices, and thus the evil works of the enemy begin to multiply.

Don't fool yourself about the damaging effects of strife. If you have illness in your body, look for all the areas where you are not in harmony with your spouse, your children, your parents, your siblings, your friends, your neighbors, your employers, your employees, etc.

At the first sign of discord, take responsibility for your thoughts, emotions, and actions, and bind every spirit of strife. Forgive quickly and walk in the love of Father God.

Father God, I am determined to end all strife in my life. I choose to be slow to get angry and quick to forgive. I will remain vigilant against allowing any form of strife to take hold in my life because I am determined to close every door to the enemy from undermining my ability to carry out Your mission and purpose for my life. In Jesus' name, I pray, Amen.

✝

Day 50
Envying Brings Confusion

For where envying and strife is, there is confusion and every evil work. (James 3:16)

For ye are yet carnal: for whereas there is among you envying, and strife, and divisions, are ye not carnal, and walk as men? (1 Corinthians 3:3)

Let us not be desirous of vain glory, provoking one another, envying one another. (Galatians 5:26)

But if ye have bitter envying and strife in your hearts, glory not, and lie not against the truth. (James 3:14)

We are starting with the same Scripture of James and this time looking at the issue of envying. When you envy someone, you want what they have.

Envy and jealousy can set up an environment for you to become sick, and then once you don't feel well, it is often magnified. You add another envy to your list when you become jealous of other people's good health. You compare your awful diagnosis from the doctor with the vitality of your friends and then allow self-pity to cry out, "Why me? It's not fair!"

These emotions lead to confusion and every evil work. The enemy wants you dead, and if he can stir up envying and strife in you, he has a good chance of succeeding. Paul reminds us that we aren't supposed to walk carnally in envy, strife, and negative emotions but spiritually in the confidence, love, and truth of the Word. Forgive quickly and don't allow yourself to entertain negative emotions.

Take authority over every thought of envy and jealousy by focusing on the finished work of the Cross. Jesus died for you. For you. His love for you is just as strong as it is for those you have been tempted to envy.

Every benefit of the Cross is yours to take, if you will just engage your will with the will of the Father. Take every gift of sozo – salvation, deliverance, doing well, healing, and being made whole. Rejoice with a heart full of gratitude for such an abundance of gifts.

Father God, I have been foolish to entertain thoughts and feelings of envy and jealousy. You have poured out so many blessings on me, Lord, that I realize that, when I am envious of someone else, I am really being ungrateful for everything You have given me. Forgive me for being so self-centered. I thank You for blessing me, Father. I am so grateful for your kindness, mercy, blessings, and covenant. In Jesus' name, I pray, Amen.

✝

DAY 51
DON'T CARRY ANGER TOWARD PEOPLE

Be ye angry, and sin not: let not the sun go down upon your wrath.
(Ephesians 4:26)

There are two different ways to interpret this verse. Today we will look at the most common view which is that Paul is telling us not to go to bed angry. Although we may experience the feeling of anger, we should not express it inappropriately or carry it longer than one day.

Anger can be similar to a momentary warning sign, like a yellow light. It flashes, we notice it, we make a decision about it, and then we release it. It's all a fairly rapid process. Once we sense a feeling of anger, it's up to us to make the choice not to keep it. Lashing out in wrath at others either verbally or physically leads only to our being controlled by the evil one.

Proverbs 16:32 reinforces this theme: "He that is slow to anger is better than the mighty; and he that ruleth his spirit than he that taketh a city." Holding onto anger is sin, yet, regrettably, most of us have a hard time letting it go. The longer we hold onto it, the stronger it gets. Some people direct their anger outward at others, and some people turn their anger inward toward themselves. Both choices lead only to pain and suffering.

Letting go of anger can be hard because you must do two things: you must take sole responsibility for nurturing it, and you must then make a conscious decision not to continue carrying it. You must face the hurt and the sorrow that lies underneath it.

Perhaps the hardest anger to deal with is anger toward God. Many of us have been angry with God, particularly for events that happened in our past. We felt that God failed to protect us and that He let us down. It is really important to acknowledge these feelings because they stand in the way of trust and faith.

Look into your heart. God already knows what is there. If you are ready to be free of your anger, be courageous enough to acknowledge it and offer it to Him. Let Him fill you with His healing love and forgiveness.

Merciful Father, sometimes I have held onto old hurts and kept anger alive. I know I have even felt angry with You and have sometimes been unwilling to trust You. I feel ashamed to admit it but it's true. Father God, I don't like myself when I allow anger to simmer and then explode on the people around me. I now take full responsibility for my emotions, and I take a stand against allowing anger and rage to control my life and steal relationships from me. I praise You for the victory won for me through the shed blood of Your Son, Jesus Christ, and I thank You for the deliverance available to me through the atonement. In the mighty name of Jesus, I pray, Amen.

✝

DAY 52
IT'S OK TO GET ANGRY WITH THE DEVIL

Be ye angry, and sin not: let not the sun go down upon your wrath.
(Ephesians 4:26)

In the previous message, we looked at the most prevalent interpretation of this verse, which is that we are to resolve all our issues of anger with other people by the end of the day. The focus of that interpretation is our anger at other people.

I heard Andrew Wommack preach an excellent message on this verse, and he suggested that there is another way to look at this Scripture, in addition to the one we have already discussed. He used this verse as a reminder that there is "righteous anger" at the enemy. We are to hate evil and to resist the enemy vigorously. We are never to let up on our opposition to him. "Don't let the sun go down upon your wrath." Don't get tired of standing against the evil one and go to bed with your defenses down.

To reinforce this, Paul says later in Ephesians, "for we wrestle not against flesh and blood, but against principalities, against powers, against the rulers of the darkness of this world, against spiritual wickedness in high places. Wherefore take unto you the whole armour of God, that ye may be able to withstand in the evil day, and having done all, to stand" (Ephesians 6:12-13). Stand, Paul tells us.

Stand. Your battle is against all the forces of darkness, and you must not allow yourself to grow weary and to fail to stand. God has given you every tool you need to stand in victory.

Righteous anger is meant to be directed at the enemy and his evil works. This doesn't mean that we are to stay stirred up emotionally, seething with anger at the devil. What having this righteous anger means is that we are supposed to see through the enemy's efforts to use other people to irritate and upset us, and realize that these people are not our enemy but that satan is. Instead of turning our anger on each other and on ourselves, we are supposed to be targeting the destroyer and taking authority over him.

Paul tells us that getting angry at the devil is not sin because we are to "abhor that which is evil" (Romans 12:9). It is vitally important to stay single-minded and persistent in our opposition to the devil's work. He has come to steal, kill, and destroy, and God has given us the responsibility and the authority through the blood of Jesus to bind him and to walk in the victory of the Cross.

Father God, I renew my intent to see through the enemy's schemes to set me in opposition to other people. I refuse to allow anger at others to take hold of me and to divert me from identifying my true enemy who is satan. Thank You for giving me all the tools, Father, to stand successfully against the devil who has come to steal, kill, and destroy. Jesus gave me power over all the power of the enemy, and I wield that authority in His name. In Jesus' name, I pray, Amen.

†
DAY 53
ARE YOU HIDING SECRETS?

But a certain man named Ananias, with Sapphira his wife, sold a possession, and kept back part of the price, his wife also being privy to it, and brought a certain part, and laid it at the apostles' feet. But Peter said, Ananias, why hath Satan filled thine heart to lie to the Holy Ghost, and to keep back part of the price of the land? Whiles it remained, was it not thine own? and after it was sold, was it not in thine own power? why hast thou conceived this thing in thine heart? thou hast not lied unto men, but unto God.

And Ananias hearing these words fell down, and gave up the ghost: and great fear came on all them that heard these things. And the young men arose, wound [wrapped] him up, and carried him out, and buried him.   (Acts 5:1-6)

This is a very powerful illustration of the fact that guilt, terror, and extreme fear kill because powerful demonic spirits accompany them. You cannot carry guilt around for long without its affecting your whole being. It will eat at you slowly but surely.

In addition to the mental and emotional stress, there is a real impact on the functioning of your immune system and on the organs of your body. Terror stresses your adrenals to their maximum limits, and sometimes the pressure put on them is too much to sustain.

THE POWER OF GOD'S WORD FOR OVERCOMING

Some people believe that God killed Ananias for lying to the church. But read this Scripture again. It says that, when Ananias heard the truth spoken and saw his deeds revealed, he fell down and died, not that God killed him.

When Peter confronted Ananias' wife, he told her what happened to her husband and prophesied that the same thing would happen to her. At that moment she, too, fell down and died from both terror and guilt.

What secrets are you hiding? Don't be deceived by the evil one into thinking that they are hidden either from God or from the cells in your body. The stress of keeping these secrets is affecting you every minute of the day and night, no matter how strong you think you might be. Sooner or later the truth will come to light, and you will have a very heavy price to pay.

Confess your sins and make atonement for them. Seek deliverance from anything that keeps you in bondage. Jesus has paid the price for you, so walk in the freedom of the Cross.

Almighty God, I don't want any sin to provide an open door for the enemy to use against me. Therefore, I confess that I have sinned, and I've made restitution as best I can. I refuse to entertain thoughts of guilt, shame, and fear. Thank You for the cleansing power of the blood of Jesus, in whose name I pray, Amen.

✝

DAY 54
GRIEF AND DEPRESSION

... and their soul shall be as a watered garden; and they shall not sorrow any more at all. Then shall the virgin rejoice in the dance, both young men and old together: for I will turn their mourning into joy, and will comfort them, and make them rejoice from their sorrow. (Jeremiah 31:12-13)

How do you handle loss, disappointment, sadness, and regrets? Some people stay locked in their grief and bound by their sorrow all their life. The wound in their soul remains unhealed, and they never engage fully with life again. Instead, they live with a piece of themselves that is dead and lifeless.

Frequently, this leads to illness and disease. Grief depresses the immune system; sorrow causes constrictions in blood vessels, decreasing blood flow to organs and cells. There are often cases of spouses who have lived many years together and who died within months of each other. The grief of the surviving spouse was so overwhelming as to have a catastrophic effect on both body and soul.

Take a look at your life. Are you carrying some sorrow or grief? It may be for a person you loved and who has died. Or it may be a sorrow for something you missed when you were growing up. It is very common for people growing up in seriously dysfunctional families to carry grief for not being loved as they needed to be loved. There is also grief for a life situation that you missed. You may have longed to be married and grieve over never having found a spouse – or you may have longed to be a parent and grieve over never having had children.

When we suffer a great loss, there is a time to mourn and to grieve. But at some point we have to move on with our lives because God's Word repeatedly says that we are to be filled with the Lord's joy. Grief can provide a hiding place and give us an excuse to withdraw from life.

It takes courage to let go of the past and to become fully engaged in the present. God has a mission and a purpose for us, and we can't fulfill it if we are looking backward to the way things were or are bemoaning the way things might have been.

If you have been imprisoned by grief for a long time, consider the possibility that spirits of grief may have taken over. If that is the case, seek deliverance and get free. God has provided for your mourning to be turned into joy.

Almighty God, I have grieved long enough. I take authority over all spirits of grief and depression and command them to leave me. I choose to give You all my burdens, Lord, so that I can move forward with gladness. Thank You for turning my mourning into joy and for giving me Your comfort. Thank You for filling my body with Your healing blessing. In the name of Your Son, Jesus Christ, I pray, Amen.

†

Day 55
What Is A Real Family?

While he yet talked to the people, behold, his mother and his brethren stood without, desiring to speak with him. Then one said unto him, Behold, thy mother and thy brethren stand without, desiring to speak with thee. But he answered and said unto him that told him, Who is my mother? and who are my brethren? And he stretched forth his hand toward his disciples, and said, Behold my mother and my brethren! For whosoever shall do the will of my Father which is in heaven, the same is my brother, and sister, and mother. (Matthew 12:46-50)

Jesus gives us a new definition of family. He didn't reject His mother or brothers, nor did He imply that they were not following the will of God. But He made it clear that He considered His family to be those believers who placed Him at the center of their lives and who did the will of the Father.

Many people find that their family and relatives are the most resistant to the God-directed healing path. You may find that the same is true for you. If you are guided to use natural substances for your healing (rather than synthetic pharmaceuticals) or to say no to standard medical treatments that destroy the immune system, those who love you may be frightened when they see you reject what they believe is the only sensible way to deal with illness. It is futile to try to change them. Pray for them to have peace concerning your choices, and pray that the Holy Spirit will give them revelation knowledge of the truths you have learned.

Remember that your focus is to do the will of God. That and only that. Find people who believe in the healing power of God and are able to support you. Bring them into your life as your family.

Another family issue happens when a person wants love and support that his blood family can't – or won't – give him. Instead of letting go, the person tries to make his family act the way he believes they should. However, relationships based on a common love of Father God and Jesus and true joy in being together are what constitute a real family.

Family is a matter of the heart and spirit, rather than of blood. Hold fast to those who support you in following God's will to the best of your ability. Embrace them, love them, and tell them how grateful you are to have them as your true family of the heart.

Gracious God, keep me strong in my resolve to follow Your path even though some of my family and friends don't understand what I am doing. Thank You for sending people to me who believe that it is Your will for me to be well and who support and help me in my healing. I am grateful for them in this journey, and I welcome them as my new family. In the name of Your Son, Jesus Christ, I pray, Amen.

†

DAY 56
THE BENEFITS OF BEING SICK

My son, attend to my words; incline thine ear unto my sayings. Let them not depart from thine eyes; keep them in the midst of thine heart. For they are life unto those that find them, and health to all their flesh. (Proverbs 4:20-22)

God's Word is filled with empowerment for His people. It is packed from beginning to end with promises that God makes to us. In order for those promises to be fulfilled, we must attend to God's Word, and we must focus completely on it. "Keep your eyes on Me," God says to us. Gaze steadfastly on Him.

Follow unswervingly God's will for you. Keep God's Word and God's promises locked deep within your heart. Remember that God has promised us that He will give us the desires of our heart. If we have our symptoms buried there instead of God's Word, we will surely reap what we sow.

Examine what is in the midst of your heart now. Oddly enough, being ill often carries benefits with it. One of those is receiving more support and love than is the case when you are well. Are you reluctant to ask your friends and family for attention when you are well and strong? Read the passages in Holy Scripture which teach about asking and learn to request the support you need.

Another benefit is that illness can be a hiding place from the world. Are you afraid of living? Do you feel you have failed to accomplish anything of value? Do you feel disconnected from the flow of life around you and that you don't fit in it or belong? Know that all these feelings and beliefs originate from the father of lies.

The truth is that you are a child of God and consequently have great value. God constantly asks you to choose life. He wants you to live in joy and in fulfillment of His purpose for you. Examining what is buried in your innermost heart can be painful. If you find beliefs that are detrimental to your emotional and physical health, acknowledge them, give them to God with repentance, and feel God's forgiveness heal you.

Let go of these old patterns that trap you, and keep only God's Word in the midst of your heart.

Almighty God, I clear away all my old beliefs and allow my innermost heart to be washed by the blood of Your Son, Christ Jesus. I focus only on Your Word and Your will for my life. I absorb Your Holy Scripture into the midst of my heart, for I know that they are life to me and health to my body. In Jesus' name, I pray, Amen.

✝

DAY 57
THE RAVAGES OF ADDICTIONS

Who hath woe? who hath sorrow? who hath contentions? who hath babbling? who hath wounds without cause? who hath redness of eyes? They that tarry long at the wine; they that go to seek mixed wine. Look not thou upon the wine when it is red, when it giveth his colour in the cup, when it moveth itself aright. At the last it biteth like a serpent, and stingeth like an adder.

Thine eyes shall behold strange women, and thine heart shall utter perverse things. Yea, thou shalt be as he that lieth down in the midst of the sea, or as he that lieth upon the top of a mast. They have stricken me, shalt thou say, and I was not sick; they have beaten me, and I felt it not: when shall I awake? I will seek it yet again. (Proverbs 23:29-35)

This passage in Proverbs vividly describes the ravages of addiction to alcohol and its disastrous consequences. There are many substances and activities, such as alcohol, mind-altering drugs, prescription drugs, tobacco, caffeine, pornography, sex, and gambling – which can take control in our lives and create dependency.

Addictive spirits are major principalities in satan's kingdom, and they work by intensifying emotional pain. The inner pain is one we are afraid to face, and we find that the addictive substance blunts the pain, allows us to hide, and gives us a momentary, illusory feeling of power or control. As long as we stay actively involved in our addiction, we can pretend to be a helpless victim, and we can avoid taking responsibility for our lives.

The addictive spirits keep us in torment and create disastrous effects on our health. To be well in our body, we also have to be healed in our soul, emotions, and mind. God has provided a complete solution for us as a part of the finished work of the Cross. Total freedom is available to us through deliverance. Emotional pain and the evil spirits behind it are confronted, confessed, and banished.

Our God is ever faithful and delivers and releases us from every addiction. He brings us liberty, breaking every tormenting bond so that we can walk the joyous path of freedom that He intended.

Loving Father, give me the courage to face my addictions and the inner wounds that I carry. I'm tired of playing the victim, so I acknowledge my sin in allowing these demonic spirits to control my life. Forgive me, Father, for letting them take hold, and help me to forgive myself. Thank You for providing deliverance through the atonement of the Cross. Help me to find other Spirit-filled believers who will help me to be diligent in renewing my mind. Lord God, I begin anew to walk more closely with You. In Jesus' name, I pray, Amen.

SECTION FOUR

HINDRANCES THAT COME FROM NOT TAKING GOD AT HIS WORD

It is crucial that we seek God
and His instructions first,
that we take God at His Word, and
that we obey Him fully and wholeheartedly.

✝

DAY 58
DO YOU TRUST GOD WITH YOUR LIFE?

Trust in the Lord with all thine heart; and lean not unto thine own understanding. In all thy ways acknowledge him, and he shall direct thy paths. (Proverbs 3:5-6)

Do you trust God with your life? The answer would seem to be obvious. But is it? It is amazing how many people do not include God in the process of making their health decisions. They pray to God for health; however, when they do so, they spend all their time talking *to* God instead of listening to what God has to say.

Scripture warns us not to "lean on *our* own understanding." Medical tests, medical opinions and scientific facts are all part of *our* understanding. They are informative input based on the knowledge and the mind of man. Sometimes the information seems to be irrevocable fact, but remember that scientific "facts" have changed constantly through the centuries (and still change today) as human beings learn more and more.

God does not have any opinions. God is divine truth, and He knows everything there is to know about your body. In fact, there are things He knows about your body that no human being will ever understand fully. Therefore, we are told not to base our decisions *solely* on man's knowledge but to seek the Lord. Take your health issues to God in prayer, quieten your mind, and be open to hear God.

If you will let Him, God can give you *very specific* advice about the best way for *you* to receive the healing He desires. He wants to share this knowledge with you. He wants to direct you to the path that is right for you. You must listen on a daily basis because the specific divine instructions may change as you follow God's path.

Remain faithful to God's voice. You may hear that you are to apply certain essential oils, take certain herbs, use certain medications, have certain medical procedures, go to church elders for healing prayer, or receive healing through deliverance. Or you may be given a combination of these pathways to healing.

Just listen. Make sure you hear the voice of God and only the voice of God. Then have faith and act boldly no matter what anyone else says.

Father God, I trust in You with all my heart, and I lean not on my own understanding. As I gather information from my family, friends, and health advisors, I choose to stand strong and to rely ultimately on Your holy guidance. When Your voice and their advice don't agree, I choose to follow You. I want You to be the one who directs my path. Thank You, Father, for Your wisdom, discernment, and strength. In Jesus' name, I pray, Amen.

✝

DAY 59
GIDEON'S FAITH WALK

And the Lord said unto Gideon, The people that are with thee are too many for me to give the Midianites into their hands, lest Israel vaunt themselves against me, saying, Mine own hand hath saved me. Now therefore go to, proclaim in the ears of the people, saying, Whosoever is fearful and afraid, let him return and depart early from mount Gilead. And there returned of the people twenty and two thousand; and there remained ten thousand.

And the Lord said unto Gideon, The people are yet too many; bring them down unto the water, and I will try them for thee there. ... Every one that lappeth of the water with his tongue, as a dog lappeth, him shalt thou set by himself ...

By the three hundred men that lapped will I save you, and deliver the Midianites into thine hand: and let all the other people go every man unto his place. ...

And the three companies blew the trumpets, and brake the pitchers, and held the lamps in their left hands, and the trumpets in their right hands to blow withal: and they cried, The sword of the Lord, and of Gideon. And they stood every man in his place round about the camp: and all the host ran, and cried, and fled. (Judges 7:2-5, 7, 20-21)

Hundreds of thousands of men strong, the Midianite army swept into Israel. Hearing the Israelites crying to be saved, God selected Gideon to crush the enemy. Gideon gathered an army of thirty-two thousand men and prepared to fight. But the Lord God Almighty told him that he had to reduce the number of his troops.

Imagine Gideon's shock when God told him that his army was too big! How could his army be too big since it was still very small compared to the army of the enemy? Pay close attention to what God said to Gideon for His reason for wanting Gideon to have a tiny army composed only of those strong in their faith. He did not want the people of Israel to boast to God that they had saved themselves. He wanted them to be clear that He and He alone was their deliverer.

When we have been attacked with sickness, we have much the same situation as Gideon. We have been invaded by the evil one. To fight him, we have developed an impressive array of weapons in conventional medical treatment – drugs, surgery, and radiation, to name a few. We have become quite boastful of our discoveries, inventions, and manipulations of chemicals. There is nothing wrong with our having these things as long as we remember that they are man-made and not God-made and, therefore, are subject to certain limitations.

Medical treatments do not actually heal because healing comes from *life* – and it is the living body which heals through the touch of the Almighty. We forget that fact and too often exalt these medical treatments to the level of God. Our immediate impulse is to employ the most powerful arsenal of drugs, chemotherapy, radiation, or surgery that we can in order to defeat our disease. We put our faith in these things without even asking God whether we should use them in our own particular situation. We utilize them without seeking God's advice or exploring God's remedies. When they work, we credit them with our recovery, and when they don't, we often blame God.

If God tells you to take action with medical treatments, then you should do it. But before you embark on any "obvious" course, go in prayer to the Lord. Seek His advice and counsel with complete willingness to obey Him. Make very sure it is His voice – and His alone – that you are following.

What if God tells you to use juniper berries, uva ursi, and astragalus to heal a bladder infection instead of high-powered antibiotic? That may seem to you like pitting three hundred men against thousands upon thousands. Are you willing to do it if God directly instructs you?

God does not want us to boast that we have saved ourselves or healed ourselves through our own treatments. "I am the God who heals you," He declares. Have the courage of Gideon to join in partnership with Him as your first resort and not as your last resort. Stand with Him in faith.

Merciful Father, let me never forget it isn't my own hand that will save me but only Your mighty power. I affirm that it is You and You alone who are my Healer. You are the source of all life, and You have sent Your Son, Jesus Christ, to purchase my total freedom through the shed blood of the Cross. By the stripes of Jesus I am healed. It is finished. It is done. I stand firm like those of Gideon's army. And I walk in complete victory because I joyously proclaim that You are more than enough! Reveal to me Your truth, and give me courage to follow Your wisdom obediently and persistently. In Jesus' mighty name, I pray, Amen.

✝

DAY 60
DO YOU HAVE BETTER ANSWERS THAN GOD?

This is what the Sovereign Lord, the Holy One of Israel, says: Only in returning to me and resting in me will you be saved. In quietness and confidence is your strength.

But you would have none of it. You said, 'No, we will get our help from Egypt. They will give us swift horses for riding into battle.' But the only swiftness you are going to see is the swiftness of your enemies chasing you! One of them will chase a thousand of you. Five of them will make all of you flee. ...

So the Lord must wait for you to come to him so he can show you his love and compassion. For the Lord is a faithful God. Blessed are those who wait for his help. (Isaiah 30:15-18 New Living Translation)

Why is it that we think we have better answers than God? Over and over again God offers solutions to our problems, but we are sure we know a better way.

Often God's answers seem impossible or ridiculous or even stupid. With an army in hot pursuit, God told his people that their strength was in quietness and confidence. But no, they relied on the appearance of the situation, trusted in their horses, and fled in fear. The only result was that their pursuers were as swift as they were.

God is constantly having to deal with human beings who are stubborn and rebellious. We become filled with arrogance, convinced that we are the creators of knowledge and truth.

Look at what has happened in the scientific field. We have told God that He does not have any place in the study of scientific "facts" and then have placed our faith in scientific theories, forgetting that they are only theories and not necessarily God's truth. We foolishly tell God to "get You out of the way" (Isaiah 30:11) because we are tired of being confronted with the Holy One of Israel! We are unwilling to listen to the Lord's instruction.

We see God warning us again in Psalm 20:7: "Some trust in chariots, and some in horses: but we will remember the name of the Lord our God." These Scriptures do not mean to refuse to use scientific and medical treatment any more than David was to reject chariots or horses. After all, they can be useful tools, even life-saving ones.

The issue is how to use them and when to use them. Most people make the decision to follow a certain medical treatment and then pray to God for a successful outcome. We are to ask God's advice first, not last.

On a wider scale, we need more people to pray for a new direction for science. We need to pray for more and more godly scientists, who will ask God first how they should explore our natural world and who will seek guidance in each step as they create. Bringing God into the creative process insures that we benefit our world instead of harming and destroying it. Your prayers can make a difference for our world and for our children's world.

God is a patient God. He is filled with compassion for us, and He wants us to be well. He has provided for our healing through the Cross. He meets us where we are in our faith, and sometimes He uses the methods we have discovered and invented. But other times He tells us "in quietness and confidence shall be your strength." Don't tell God, "I will have none of it." Say instead, "Yes, Lord, I hear You and I will obey."

Almighty God, thank You for being patient with me. I have been rebellious and I am sorry. I want to manifest my healing, and I am willing to listen to You and to follow Your instructions. Guide me, and I will be obedient. Give me the strength to stop following the opinions of others blindly and instead to ask Your advice and to make Your answer my final one. In the name of Your Son, Jesus Christ, my Savior and my Redeemer, I pray, Amen.

✝

DAY 61
WHAT SEEMS "RIGHT" MAY LEAD TO DEATH

There is a way that seems right to a man and appears straight before him, but at the end of it is the way of death. (Proverbs 16:25 Amplified Bible)

It is interesting that this verse is repeated again in Proverbs 14:12. Often when health problems hit us, we find we are on "the way of death," even though we had thought we were doing the "right" thing. The root of the problem is our failure to include God as a full partner in each of our decisions. We hand over responsibility for our health to scientists and to government "authorities" and follow their pronouncements instead of taking their recommendations to God before acting.

Edward Jenner discovered the technique of vaccinations for smallpox in 1796, and we continue to develop massive numbers of vaccines. Almost every year, a new vaccine is hailed as the solution to a current health problem. This news is particularly seductive because having a simple shot means no one has to change what he is doing – or ask God for guidance.

Large numbers of vaccines are now administered to our children. By the age of six, most American children have received more than twenty-five, the first being given before a newborn is two days old. Unfortunately, no one really knows all of the cumulative effects of these numerous vaccines. We do know that larger and larger numbers of children are experiencing autism, asthma, allergies, ear infections, and other problems. In addition, the increase of auto-immune disorders afflicting adults may be a result of mutated viruses received from childhood vaccinations.

We now eat genetically engineered foods, most without our knowledge or consent. The motivation for such changes is generally economic – to create high yields of produce that can sit in warehouses and on grocery store shelves for weeks and even months without rotting. What arrogance! What roads to death are we paving for ourselves and for our children?

The point of God's Word in Proverbs is that you must not follow any human being *unquestioningly*. Make inquiries. Seek the "facts." Then take this information to God in prayer and follow only Him.

Almighty God, I pray for all scientists and ask that they be filled with and directed by Your Holy Spirit. Touch them so that they desire to work with You in harmony with Your will and plan for humankind. Give me the courage to speak out where I see our future compromised by harmful practices. Let me not be complaisant so that my right to follow Your guidance is taken away from me by an unwise government. Help me to listen to the guidance of the Holy Spirit. In Jesus' name, I pray, Amen.

†

Day 62
Seeking Doctors
Instead Of The Lord

And Asa in the thirty and ninth year of his reign was diseased in his feet, until his disease was exceeding great: yet in his disease he sought not to the Lord, but to the physicians. And Asa slept with his fathers, and died in the one and fortieth year of his reign. (2 Chronicles 16:12-13)

Asa had a history of relying on human effort, strength, and plans rather than on the Lord God Almighty. Most of us are more like Asa than we would like to acknowledge, especially when we feel ill. We would be wise to heed Holy Scripture and to learn from it.

Notice that this story does *not* say that Asa died because he went to doctors when he was sick. What Scripture says is that Asa "sought not to the Lord, but to the physicians." In other words, he chose the doctors *instead* of God. He depended totally on the physicians. God is a jealous God and demands to have top priority. "Thou shalt have no other gods before me" (Exodus 20:3), He says, and that includes the god of medicine.

What God intends is for us to join in full partnership with Him for our recovery. God is the source of all our healing, and we must turn to Him *first*. We must seek His direction and guidance in each step of our healing process and follow exactly what we are told to do.

When the Holy Spirit tells you to seek out a doctor or a health care practitioner, find one who will pray with you. Find one who is open to using natural substances which God has provided instead of limiting his recommendations only to man-made substances. Find one who is willing to tell you all the options available for your healing – and not only pharmaceutical or surgical ones.

Find one who truly practices the statement ascribed to Hippocrates, the Father of Medicine, "Whenever a doctor cannot do good, he must be kept from doing harm." Find one who is willing to support you in following your best understanding of God's plan for your healing.

Make sure that you place the Great Physician first in your heart, your soul, your life, and your healing program.

Almighty Father, I declare that You are the Great Physician and that You are first in my life. You are the God who heals me, and it is Your guidance that I seek. If I am to receive medical treatment, help me to find godly doctors who will pray with me and seek to work in partnership with You for my recovery. I stand on Your Holy Word, and thank You for healing me. Again and again I proclaim that by His stripes I am healed. In gratitude and praise, I pray in the name of Your Son, Jesus Christ, Amen.

✝

Day 63
The Example of David's Trust

Blessed is he who has regard for the weak; the Lord delivers him in times of trouble. The Lord will protect him and preserve his life; he will bless him in the land and not surrender him to the desire of his foes.

The Lord will sustain him on his sickbed and restore him from his bed of illness. I said, "O Lord, have mercy on me; heal me, for I have sinned against you." ...

All my enemies whisper together against me; they imagine the worst for me, saying, "A vile disease has beset him; he will never get up from the place where he lies." Even my close friend, whom I trusted, he who shared my bread, has lifted up his heel against me.

But you, O Lord, have mercy on me; raise me up, that I may repay them. I know that you are pleased with me, for my enemy does not triumph over me. In my integrity you uphold me and set me in your presence forever. Praise be to the Lord, the God of Israel, from everlasting to everlasting. Amen and Amen. (Psalm 41:1-4, 7-13 New International Version)

This is a fascinating psalm of David, who has become sick and who is praying to God for help and healing. He does not have the finished work of the Cross to rely upon, yet notice that he assumes that God will heal him. He very firmly declares, "The Lord will sustain him on his sickbed and restore him from his bed of illness." He does not doubt either God's power or God's desire to heal him.

He makes a very interesting confession. "Heal me," he says, *"for I have sinned against you."* He admits that he has violated some of God's laws – whether they be physical laws of good health or whether they be spiritual ones that make a person vulnerable to attacks of the evil one – and that he is now suffering the consequences of his actions. Illness has overcome him and he needs healing.

David raises another vital issue in healing concerning the opinions of others. He says his enemies are "imagining the worst." And even his closest friend isn't giving him his support. You, too, may find that your friends and family are focused on the worst and are filled with thoughts of fear about you. Refuse to accept their negative view of your situation; instead, choose to be like David and focus on the healing power of Jehovah-Rapha. Remain firm in your belief that you are healed by the stripes of Jesus.

Dear Heavenly Father, I relate well to the psalm of David. Some people around me are imagining the worst about my illness, but help me to stay focused on Your Word which is filled with promises of Your covenant as my healer. I know I am forgiven. I know I am saved. And I know that I am healed by the stripes of Jesus. I receive the manifestation of my healing now. In Jesus' name, I pray, Amen.

✝

DAY 64
DO YOU BELIEVE JESUS CAN HEAL YOU?

And when Jesus departed thence, two blind men followed him, crying, and saying, Thou son of David, have mercy on us. ... and Jesus saith unto them, Believe ye that I am able to do this? They said unto him, Yea, Lord. Then touched he their eyes, saying, According to your faith be it unto you. And their eyes were opened; and Jesus straitly charged them, saying, See that no man know it. (Matthew 9:27-30)

Here is a short, simple story of Jesus as He healed two blind men. We don't know from this Scripture what had caused each of the men's blindness. What scientific explanations would we use today? Glaucoma? Macular degeneration? Diabetes? Injury? Blindness is as frightening a diagnosis today as it was in Jesus' time. Think about going to a doctor who has vast knowledge about eyes and hearing him say, "I'm sorry. You're going blind. There is no known cure. Maybe we can try some new procedures or drugs." What do you do now?

You have to put aside your emotional feelings of fear and despair. You even have to put aside your logic (remember Noah). What you must do now is to go to God in prayer, meditation, and silence. Be open to God's voice and *only* God's voice so that you can hear clearly what God has to say.

Satan loves to deceive us. He especially loves to get us to equate scientific fact based on the knowledge and mind of man with divine fact based on the wisdom and mind of God. He loves to get us to believe only in the tangible "facts" that we can see and hear and touch. He wants us to believe that all test results are conclusive.

When the blind men came to him, Jesus asked, "Do you believe I can do this?" What is your answer today? Do you believe in the power of your illness or do you believe in the power of God? Do you believe that science defines reality for you? Your healing depends on what you believe and what (and who) you trust.

"According to your faith be it unto you," Jesus said. Go to God in faith and in quietness. Go to God believing that He wants you to be well. Go to God believing that He has provided healing for you through the finished work of the Cross. Resist the attack of the enemy; speak to your mountain, and command it to be removed, in the name of Jesus. Receive your healing now.

Father God, when I feel overwhelmed by man's reality, help me to see myself with Your eyes. I believe that You have already provided that I be totally well. I believe that by the stripes of Jesus Christ, I am healed. I love You, Father, and give You all the praise, honor, and glory. In the mighty name of Jesus, I pray, Amen.

†

DAY 65
DOUBT IS DEADLY

But let him ask in faith, nothing wavering. For he that wavereth is like a wave of the sea driven with the wind and tossed. For let not that man think that he shall receive any thing of the Lord. A double minded man is unstable in all his ways. (James 1:6-8)

James was the half-brother of Jesus, and he well knew the pitfalls of doubt. Doubt can tie you into knots of indecision and render you impotent and paralyzed with fear.

James describes it so well, "He who doubts is like a wave of the sea, driven with the wind and tossed." Doubting saps your strength, depresses your immune system, and makes you vulnerable to disease. As the tool of the devil, doubt hinders faith from taking action.

If you are being tormented by doubt about some decision in your life, you have fallen victim to satan's seductive whispers. Unfortunately, it often happens that you find yourself in uncertainty because you didn't ask God for guidance at the very beginning of your difficulty. You just forged ahead using your own judgment and found yourself deeper in trouble.

There are times you may have asked for God's help, yet you missed the point that James emphasizes. You must ask *believing.* "Therefore I say unto you, What things soever ye desire, when ye pray, believe that ye receive them, and ye shall have them" (Mark 11:24). However, this is possible if you ask only for those things which God promises in His Word.

It is written that Jehovah-Rapha is the God who heals you (Exodus 15:26). It is written that Christ Jesus bore your infirmities in your place (Matthew 8:17). Therefore, believe that your healing has already been provided for you.

If you seek healing but are not really sure whether it is God's will that you be well or not, then your doubt controls you. James is very blunt about the results you can expect. "That man should not think he will receive anything from the Lord."

Do not let satan destroy your life and your relationship with God through doubt and unbelief. Trust God with your health and with all your decisions.

Almighty God, I give You all my doubts and unbelief and declare my faith in You and in Your Holy Word. I do not want to be double-minded, but instead, I want to be clearly focused on You and You alone. I believe. Help me where I have areas of unbelief. Thank You for loving, guiding, and healing me. In Jesus' name, I pray, Amen.

✝

DAY 66
ARE YOU WAVERING IN INDECISION?

And Elijah came unto all the people, and said, How long halt ye between two opinions? If the Lord be God, follow him: but if Baal, then follow him. And the people answered him not a word. (1 Kings 18:21)

This is a fascinating question. "How long will you waver between two opinions?" Only one of them is from the true God, the One and Only Most High Lord God Almighty.

When you feel sick, you are given many opinions. Some come from family and friends, some come from natural health professionals, but many come from the medical profession. Even though these ideas are usually presented as facts, do not forget that they are really opinions. This is illustrated if you choose to see a second doctor, which is called seeking a second "opinion."

Why is this important to understand? Because the thing that matters most is not opinion but the *truth* of God Almighty. For medical problems most people go to the doctor, get a medical opinion, follow it, and see what happens.

Too often the first time people call on God is just before they undergo treatment or surgery, asking for God's help. Yet they never asked God whether they should have had that treatment or surgery in the first place. Few go to God in prayer in every step along the way from the first decision to the last.

When God's truth is not sought at *every* step, we are wide open for satan to slip in and begin working his destruction against us. Usually it is only after medical procedures fail to cure us, treatments create other health problems, or we are sent home to die that we turn fully to God.

It is God's will for you to be well. Medical treatment may be a part of God's direction for your healing. But you will never know if you elevate medical authority to be equal with God's. Don't waver between two opinions. Go to God first and at every step along the way. Ask Him to speak to you. Ask the Holy Spirit to fill you clearly with God's truth, instructing you about the actions to take so that your healing is fully manifested at the physical level.

Father God, You are my ultimate authority. It is Your truth which I seek. I know Your will for me which is that I be well. I want every suggestion I follow to be in accordance with Your will and Your guidance. I make a commitment to ask You at every step of the way from this day forward, and I ask for the courage to follow your direction, especially if it is different from the opinion of others. In Jesus' name, I pray, Amen.

†

DAY 67
PRAYING WITHOUT REAL BELIEF

Peter therefore was kept in prison: but prayer was made without ceasing of the church unto God for him.

And when Herod would have brought him forth, the same night Peter was sleeping between two soldiers, bound with two chains: and the keepers before the door kept the prison. And, behold, the angel of the Lord came upon him, and a light shined in the prison: and he smote Peter on the side, and raised him up, saying, Arise up quickly. And his chains fell off from his hands. ...

And he went out, and followed him; and wist not that it was true which was done by the angel; but thought he saw a vision. ... Forthwith the angel departed from him. And when Peter was come to himself, he said, Now I know of a surety, that the Lord hath sent his angel, and hath delivered me out of the hand of Herod, and from all the expectation of the people of the Jews.

And when he had considered the thing, he came to the house of Mary the mother of John, ... where many were gathered together praying. And as Peter knocked at the door of the gate, a damsel came to hearken, named Rhoda. And when she knew Peter's voice, she opened not the gate for gladness, but ran in, and told how Peter stood before the gate.

And they said unto her, Thou art mad. But she constantly affirmed that it was even so. Then said they, It is his angel. But Peter continued knocking: and when they had opened the door, and saw him, they were astonished.   (Acts 12:5-7, 9-16)

This account of the way God rescued Peter from prison is amazing, but what is even more interesting is the response of the believers who were supposedly standing and praying in faith for his release. Through the miraculous intervention of an angel, Peter was set free. It is so spectacular that even Peter thought maybe he was dreaming – until he realized that he really was free.

He showed up at John's mother's house where many believers were "praying without ceasing" for his release. Yet notice that Rhoda was the only one who accepted from the beginning that Peter had returned to them from prison. Why was that? All the Christians were "praying without ceasing," but they seemed to have the same problem that many of us do. They had faith and yet they had unbelief also.

Rhoda was the only one of all those who were praying who was single-minded in her faith so that when she saw Peter at the door, she didn't doubt it was really him. When she reported that Peter was actually outside the door, the others told her that she was crazy. They refused to believe her even though she kept insisting that it really was Peter. Finally after Peter kept banging on the door, they opened it and let him in.

Apparently, those Christians were praying because it was the thing to do, but they didn't really believe in their hearts that a miracle would happen. If they had truly been open to receive a miracle, they would have shouted, "I knew it! I knew Peter would show up here somehow!" and they would have run immediately to let him in.

How do you pray for your healing? Like the Christians at Mary's house with unbelief weighing down your faith? Or like Rhoda, with real belief in your heart? When you see the first evidence of healing in your body, do you say, "I must be out of my mind" and question it? If so, the healing that has already been released toward you may slip through your fingers. Stand in faith and receive your healing.

Father God, I believe. Help thou my unbelief. I come against unbelief now and remove every thought that supports and nurtures it. I take every thought captive and allow nothing to undermine my faith in You and in Your Holy Word. Let me be single-minded in my trust and faith in You so that I may manifest the healing that You have given me. In Jesus' name, I pray, Amen.

†

DAY 68
BE CAREFUL WHO YOU CONFIDE IN

And he went out from thence, and came into his own country; and his disciples follow him. And when the sabbath day was come, he began to teach in the synagogue: and many hearing him were astonished, saying, From whence hath this man these things? and what wisdom is this which is given unto him, that even such mighty works are wrought [performed] by his hands? Is not this the carpenter, the son of Mary, the brother of James, and Joses, and of Judah, and Simon? And are not his sisters here with us? And they were offended at him.

But Jesus said unto them, A prophet is not without honour, but in his own country, and among his own kin, and in his own house. And he could there do no mighty work, save that he laid his hands upon a few sick folk, and healed them. And he marveled because of their unbelief.   (Mark 6:1-6)

The hometown people of Nazareth were sure that they knew who Jesus was. Everyone knew He was Mary's son, but many of them questioned who His father really was. He was a brother, a carpenter, one of the hometown boys. Now here He was going around teaching, preaching, expressing ideas that astounded them, and even doing miracles. What had happened to the person they thought they knew? Many were confused, angry, and afraid.

Consequently, their fear and lack of faith held them back. The result was that Jesus was limited in what He could do. In other places, He healed large numbers of sick people, but in Nazareth He was able to perform only a few healings.

Do not be discouraged if some, or even all, of your friends and family don't support you in walking a God-directed path to recovery. You will be saying new things and taking different actions. Those people you love the most are used to the "old" you, and it is typical for them to say, "But you are taking your life in your own hands." They often can't understand that for the first time you are taking responsibility for your health and giving your life totally to the care and guidance of God.

Learn to discern who to talk to about your health situation. Be silent or vague when necessary. Don't try to convince anyone to accept what you are doing. Instead, seek out those who *can* support you in following God's guidance. Hold to your faith and give Jesus full honor in your house.

Father God, bring people into my life to support me in my healing journey. Help my family and friends to understand that I now choose to keep my house a place that gives full honor to Your Son. Thank You for giving me strength to follow Your guidance for the healing of my temple. In Jesus' name, I pray, Amen.

†

Day 69
Unconventional Ways To Victory

And it came to pass at the seventh time, when the priests blew with the trumpets, Joshua said unto the people, Shout; for the Lord hath given you the city. ... So the people shouted when the priests blew with the trumpets: and it came to pass, when the people heard the sound of the trumpet, and the people shouted with a great shout, that the wall fell down flat, so that the people went up into the city, every man straight before him, and they took the city. (Joshua 6:16, 20)

Do you have the faith of Joshua? It is important to notice how often the stories in Holy Scripture reveal God's asking His people to take actions that were completely unconventional – and often seemingly ridiculous.

Here we see Joshua at war. God tells him to march around Jericho and on the seventh day on the seventh lap to blow the trumpets and to shout. What an absurd requirement! It is as ridiculous as building a boat for a flood when there has never been rain. Or putting blood on your door so the angel of death will pass over. Or putting mud or saliva on your eyes in order to recover your sight.

It is written in the Old Testament that God often referred to His people as "stiff-necked" and "stubborn" and "disobedient." In many ways we are far worse now because we insist on holding everything up to the standard of "science" and "reality." Generally, science is defined as being totally separated from God and all things spiritual. It reveals the "facts" through "impartial" tests and the application of scientific principles. Of course, we conveniently ignore our history of changing these "facts" and principles as our understanding changes. For example, there was a time when scientists were adamantly convinced that it was a fact that the sun revolved around the earth.

How can we have gotten to the place where the very definition of science eliminates any involvement by God? That is so tragic. How have we allowed our study of the human body and how it functions to be stripped from any consideration of the Creator who made it?

Surely, we should be ever mindful that we are not God. When we exalt ourselves to the status of God and proclaim that something will happen or not happen based on a set of test results or scientific experiments, we have fallen into the trap of the evil one.

We are supposed to think and to create, but we ought to make certain that our explorations are always under the constant guidance of God. Instead of "using the minds God gave us," why don't we allow God to use our minds by letting the Holy Spirit work through us for the betterment of all people? We need to draw our conclusions with the caveat that our understanding is always very limited when compared to the understanding of God. This allows us to put the appearance of things into perspective while looking beyond to God's divine reality and truth.

All "facts" are based on the understanding of the mind of man. God gave us intelligence, not just for us to use, but for *Him* to use. Although He gave us curiosity to seek and to discover and to invent, He constantly reminds us that He exceeds anything we can possibly imagine and that His truth and power is never bound by any rules, theories, or "facts" that we may proclaim. We are always to make Him a partner in whatever we do.

Father God, I put aside my assumptions that my treatment and recovery has to be a certain way. Help me to be like Joshua, to listen for Your voice, and then to follow Your instructions exactly as You give them. I am willing to take action, to be bold, and to stand firm. I know that by the stripes of Jesus I am healed, and I rejoice in Your declaration that Your Word never returns to You void. I praise You and glorify You, Father. In Jesus' mighty name, I pray, Amen.

✝

Day 70
Obey The Instructions
Of The Lord

And it came to pass, that, as the people pressed upon him to hear the word of God, he stood by the lake of Gennesaret, and saw two ships standing by the lake: but the fishermen were gone out of them, and were washing their nets. And he entered into one of the ships, which was Simon's, and prayed him that he would thrust out a little from the land. And he sat down, and taught the people out of the ship.

Now when he had left speaking, he said unto Simon, Launch out into the deep, and let down your nets for a draught. And Simon answering said unto him, Master, we have toiled all the night, and have taken nothing: nevertheless at thy word I will let down the net. And when they had this done, they inclosed a great multitude of fishes: and their net brake. And they beckoned unto their partners, which were in the other ship, that they should come and help them. And they came, and filled both the ships, so that they began to sink. (Luke 5:1-7)

Here is another example of the results of obeying the Lord no matter how strange His instructions seem to be. Because we do not understand methods of fishing in Jesus' time in Galilee, we miss the significance of this passage.

Simon Peter had been fishing in his normal way - at night near shore in shallow water with two boats which dragged a net between them. However, Jesus tells him to do the exact opposite – to go out in the daytime to deep water with one boat to catch fish. Look at the reply of Simon Peter to Jesus' suggestion. He tells Jesus that they have fished the way they usually did, but they were unsuccessful.

Nevertheless, Peter had three important characteristics. He had an open mind, he had faith in Jesus, and he had the willingness to follow the guidance he was given. Look at the results. So many fish were caught that he needed another boat and, even then, the catch was so huge that the boats began to sink under the weight of all the fish.

Are you willing to put your life on the line and follow the example of this story? Do you live in fear that you have to treat your illness according to "the way it is always done" or are you open and willing to hear the guidance of the Lord? God wants you to be well. Allow Him to speak to you and to reveal to you the way to the manifestation of your healing. It may be contrary to every method you have ever heard of, but, if it is God's path, be willing to act with the faith of Simon.

Father God, too often I want to hold to the safety of old ways and old patterns. Open my ears so that I may hear Your voice clearly. Give me the courage to put my boat out into the deep water of faith and follow Your instructions so that the healing won for me on the Cross will be manifested in my body. In Jesus' name, I pray, Amen.

†

Day 71
Let The Lord Direct Your Steps

A man's heart deviseth his way: but the Lord directeth his steps.
(Proverbs 16:9)

For ye have need of patience, that, after ye have done the will of God, ye might receive the promise.   (Hebrews 10:36)

Who has control of your life? Is it God? Or is it yourself? What course do you follow when you feel sick? God's? Or your own? We need to get clear that our steps should be determined by God and God alone because we can become deceived very easily.

For example, sometimes what looks like illness is, in fact, really the cure. A good illustration is the common cold. With this ailment, our immune system has become weakened (which is the real problem) and a virus has taken hold inside our body. We start sneezing, our eyes water, our nose fills with mucus and becomes clogged, and we cough. In short, we feel awful. God has created the body to take all these actions to rid itself of the virus. Since the body has gone into appropriate action to remove the germ, the cold symptoms are not the disease; they are the cure.

But what do most people do? They follow their own (erroneous) understanding and take every medicine they can to suppress the symptoms that are annoying and unpleasant. By focusing on the symptoms and trying to

213

eliminate them, they are not dealing effectively with meeting the needs of their body according to the steps that God has determined.

Instead, what is the proper solution? Let God determine your steps so that you can strengthen your immune system as quickly as possible and, thus, allow your body to restore its proper function.

Command every cold virus to leave you in the name of Jesus. Command your immune system to be strong and to function properly. Then go to God in prayer for guidance. Every born-again believer has been given the Holy Spirit as Comforter, Counselor, and Guide. Jesus wants you to have immediate access to truth, so every answer you need can be found in the Holy Spirit who dwells within.

So ask the Holy Spirit to reveal to you any action you are to take at the physical realm. You may be guided to use God's own herbal remedies and essential oils. There are many ways to assist your body to be strong and healthy, and the Holy Spirit will provide the guidance that is right for you.

If your healing doesn't manifest instantaneously, then hold onto the encouragement of the writer of Hebrews to do the will of God, be patient, and expect the fulfillment of the promise. What a faith-builder that Scripture is! If we stay focused on God's Word by acting on the Word, we will receive the promise. It is up to us to do what the Word says to do – to bind attacks of the enemy in the name of Jesus, to command our bodies to function normally, to take proper physical care of our temple, to proclaim the Word in faith, and to know that we have already received our healing.

Give God total control in your life. Do not make assumptions for your healing. Allow God to determine your steps, knowing that He wants only good for you.

Almighty God, there are times when I become willful and stubborn. I pretend that I am in control, and I charge ahead without asking You for direction first. Slow me down, Father. I trust You to guide me along the path to my recovery that is for my highest good. You, and only You, are my healer. I make a decision to follow Your will and Your instructions patiently as I progress to full recovery. In Jesus' name, I pray, Amen.

✝

DAY 72
DON'T DIE BEFORE YOUR TIME

Be not over much wicked, neither be thou foolish: why shouldest thou die before thy time? (Ecclesiastes 7:17)

Why die before your time? God wants you to fulfill all your days. He wants you to fulfill His purpose for your life. Here in Ecclesiastes it is put clearly before us that it is usually up to us whether we die before our time. Notice the two things that are listed as the major sources of dying before our time – either being too wicked or being too foolish. Aren't these interesting reasons?

The health consequences of being foolish are myriad and obvious. If we live on hamburgers and French fries, we open the door to develop heart disease. If we gorge ourselves on candy and sweets, we set ourselves up for diabetes. If we breathe in smoke, we are inviting lung problems, such as emphysema.

Many diseases are a result of our own foolishness and stubbornness. They are not the result of God's will but of *our* own will and our determination to do just exactly what we want – when we want to do it. There is a price to pay, but often that accounting does not occur until years and even decades of abuse. We lie to ourselves and think that we are getting away with our actions. Led further and further astray by the father of lies, we end up trapped and ill.

The health consequences of being sinful are less obvious. When we have anger and bitterness in our hearts, our bodies are affected. When we are filled with desire for revenge, our bodies are affected. When we gloat over taking advantage of others, our bodies are affected.

None of these negative emotions are godly. They are tools of the evil one, and they set up an internal environment for illness. The more quickly we recognize that we are out of step with God, the more quickly we can repent, ask forgiveness, get deliverance, and get back into harmony with God.

Do not choose to die before your time. Repent, ask for forgiveness, and make the changes you need to make in your life so that you may fulfill your days.

Almighty God, I'm sorry for all the things that I've done that I shouldn't have done, and I am sorry for not doing those things that I should have done. I repent of my sins and ask forgiveness. I take responsibility for allowing feelings of bitterness, resentment, grief, and fear to control my life. Warn me when I am being foolish and help me to walk with You in joy and obedience. I seek to be closer and closer to You so that I may follow Your will for me. In the name of Christ Jesus, my Savior and my Redeemer, I pray, Amen.

†

Day 73
Hearing God Clearly

Beloved, believe not every spirit, but try the spirits whether they are of God: because many false prophets are gone out into the world. Hereby know ye the Spirit of God: Every spirit that confesseth that Jesus Christ is come in the flesh is of God: And every spirit that confesseth not that Jesus Christ is come in the flesh is not of God. (1 John 4:1-3)

Many people die before their time because they think they are hearing from God when they really are not. We know that we must go to God in prayer, listen to His voice, and follow the instructions we are given. But can we trust everything that we "hear"? How can we tell the difference between God's voice and satan's voice?

This problem was well understood by the early Christians. We are warned to "test the spirits to see whether they are from God" and to "prove all things" (1 Thessalonians 5:21). Why? Because when you pray for advice and counsel, you want to make sure that the enemy isn't already perched on your shoulder ready to whisper his lies and deceptions in your ear.

God cannot contradict Himself. Therefore, whatever you hear must line up with the Word of God if it is really God's voice.

For example, God's Word says clearly that "by His stripes we were healed." Therefore, if the voice you hear tells you repeatedly that "I'm teaching you a lesson, but I may heal you someday," then that simply is not God. Usually such messages are accompanied by some instruction that is not for your good. God's healing power is already released toward you through the shed blood of the Cross, so He cannot tell you that He might do something later that He has already done.

Think about this for a moment. God has given you the faith you need. If your faith is fully developed and you are attacked by an illness, then you will take action against the enemy and receive your healing and the manifestation of it from the Lord. If your faith level is less developed, who wants you to die while you are standing on your faith? Certainly not God. He wills for you to live to His glory. But satan would be delighted to take you out by giving you bad advice.

Hold everything you hear up to the light of the Word and the light of the finished work of the Cross. Take authority over every thought, and pray for wisdom, discernment, and clarity. Learn to recognize your Master's voice.

Father God, I want to hear You and only You. I will try the spirits as I am instructed to do by the Apostle John because I don't want to be deceived. I am one of Your sheep and I do hear Your voice. I am going to press in closer to You so that nothing hinders my hearing You clearly. In the name of Your Son, Jesus Christ, I pray, Amen.

✝

DAY 74
TAKE ACTION IN OBEDIENCE

Then said Martha unto Jesus, Lord, if thou hadst been here, my brother had not died. But I know, that even now, whatsoever thou wilt ask of God, God will give it thee. ... Jesus said, Take ye away the stone. Martha, the sister of him that was dead, saith unto him, Lord, by this time he stinketh: for he hath been dead four days.

Jesus saith unto her, Said I not unto thee, that, if thou wouldest believe, thou shouldest see the glory of God? ... And when he thus had spoken, he cried with a loud voice, Lazarus, come forth. And he that was dead came forth, bound hand and foot with graveclothes; and his face was bound about with a napkin. Jesus saith unto them, Loose him, and let him go.
(John 11:21-22, 39-40, 43-44)

Have you ever wondered why Jesus asked the mourners at Lazarus' tomb to take away the stone? Surely it would have been just as easy for Jesus to have rolled the stone away as to raise Lazarus from the dead. Jesus was teaching both the mourners and us a very important lesson: we have to take a step of faith.

We have to be willing to listen, and we have to be willing to act on the guidance that we hear. Since Jesus was standing beside Martha, talking to her, it was very easy for her to hear Him with her ears. She knew Him, she trusted

Him, she loved Him, and she had seen Him heal other people.

Yet when He gave her the first instruction, she objected because she thought that her brother had been dead too long. But Jesus asked her to trust, to have faith, and to take action according to His instructions, even if it did not make sense to her.

We have not seen Jesus in the flesh as Martha did. Actually, Jesus spoke an even greater blessing on us because of that fact. "Thomas, because thou hast seen me, thou hast believed: blessed are they that have not seen, and yet have believed" (John 20:29).

When illness strikes, we have to take action and not move into a passive state, pleading with God to do everything. God has already moved. He sent His Son to the Cross to purchase our salvation, healing, and deliverance. Now we must act. We must enforce the Word of God by speaking it over our bodies and by reading it daily. The more time we spend planting good seeds of faith, the easier it is to believe God's truth that by His stripes we are healed.

Father God, You teach me once again to take action. I step out boldly to follow every instruction of the Holy Spirit. I move forward as I joyfully proclaim that I am healed by the stripes of Jesus. I act in faith, knowing that Your Word is always true. In Jesus' name, I pray, Amen.

†

DAY 75
TAKE CONTROL OVER EVERY THOUGHT

Casting down imaginations, and every high thing that exalteth itself against the knowledge of God, and bringing into captivity every thought to the obedience of Christ. (2 Corinthians 10:5)

A few words of Paul in his second letter to the Corinthians capture one of the most difficult tasks of all – to bring every thought into captivity to the obedience of Christ. When we feel ill, it is very easy to let our imaginations run wild. Having heard the information presented by medical authorities, our minds are quickly flooded with all kinds of terrible scenarios. The "what-ifs" take over, and we are embedded in doubt and confusion.

This is the evil one at work. Satan is the one who exalts himself against the knowledge of God. He wants to keep us from accessing that knowledge, from listening, and from receiving divine guidance. His mission is to whisper thoughts in our mind and convince us to accept those thoughts as our own. He wants to keep us immersed in our thoughts so that our brain stays busy seeking to find its own answers. As long as we stay focused on our own ideas, doubts, and concerns, we can't simultaneously be focused on God's ideas, plans, and truth.

God wants us to be well and whole, and He has already purchased it for us through the blood of Jesus. God does not want us to be imagining horrible physical conditions or disastrous emotional situations. It is always His desire that we be free to walk with Him and His Son, Jesus Christ, rather than to be enslaved by the evil one.

If you want to be well, take Paul's exhortation to heart. Give full attention to guarding the doors of your mind just as vigorously as you would work to keep snakes out of your living room. Do not let satan have easy occupancy, but remain vigilant and throw him out whenever you realize that he has sneaked back in.

The requirement is the same now as it has always been – obedience. We must be willing to seek God, to listen to His voice, and to obey Him. He demands that we give no opinions, thoughts, or ideas any weight which are not in full agreement with His Word.

Merciful Heavenly Father, I cast down imaginations and every high thing that exalts itself against the knowledge of You, and I bring into captivity every thought to the obedience of Christ. I want only Your voice in my heart and my mind. I want only Your guidance. I renew my resolve to examine every thought that I think, and I freely surrender my own will to Your plan and purpose for my life. In Jesus' name, I pray, Amen.

†

Day 76
Renew Your Mind

And be not conformed to this world: but be ye transformed by the renewing of your mind, that ye may prove what is that good, and acceptable, and perfect, will of God.   (Romans 12:2)

Paul warns us not to be conformed to this world because we would be led astray. That is certainly true today in the area of health.

The way of the world supports little true healing. We are flooded with advertisements for drugs which are available by prescription only because of their strong potential for harm. They are designed to eliminate symptoms rather than to heal the root cause of illness. We are encouraged to have body parts removed rather than to cleanse and nourish them so that they may recover their normal function. We are enticed with a myriad of "instant" remedies.

All these patterns of the world seduce us into accepting the temporary appearance of healing instead of true healing. The easy answers advocated usually require few changes in our food, our way of living, or our thoughts.

God wants you to be healthy. Renew your mind by reading Holy Scripture to see what God says about good health.   God requires your complete attention and commitment. When you renew your mind, you let go of your childish desire to do everything you used to do and still be healthy. That is what produced a spiritual and physical environment in your body in which disease could live in the first place.

Through renewal, you accept responsibility for your part in creating an environment for illness to flourish, and you are transformed. Through renewal, you make the commitment to follow healthy living principles, and you are transformed.

Through renewal, you forgive yourself for your mistakes, and you are transformed. Through renewal, you change your thoughts to ones which support recovery and health, and you are transformed. Through renewal, you praise God for healing you, even if you don't yet see its manifestation in your body, and you are transformed.

Look at the magnificent promise that, if you accept your responsibility to renew your mind, you will prove what is the good, acceptable, and perfect will of God.

Gracious, loving Father, I confess that I have blindly followed the patterns of this world, and my mind and body have paid a heavy price for it. I now choose not to let the world mold me, but instead I take charge of my mind by renewing it through Your Word. I want You in complete control of my life. In the name of Your Son, Jesus, I pray, Amen.

✝

DAY 77
GOD STRENGTHENS YOU

I can do all things through Christ which strengtheneth me.
(Philippians 4:13)

Paul had been imprisoned, beaten, stoned, shipwrecked, robbed, hungry, and cold. Certainly, he had endured far more tribulations than most people ever encounter in one lifetime.

Despite all these hardships, here he is proclaiming that "I can do all things through Christ which strengtheneth me." He knew that there was no attack powerful enough to separate him from the love of God and Jesus Christ. As long as Paul kept his eyes focused steadfastly on his Risen Lord, he would emerge victorious.

The source of illness is the evil one. When you are attacked in your body, look to Christ Jesus for your strength and for your healing. You can do all things with the help of the Lord if you are willing to do your part.

You must be willing to see how you have allowed yourself to become vulnerable to satan's attack and look for the ways that you contributed to your situation. What things could you have done differently to keep your body and immune system strong and more resistant to infection and disease? Ask the Holy Spirit to reveal to you anything you may have overlooked.

While you are in the process of recovery, do not focus on all the negative aspects of your situation. Paul said that he had "learned, in whatsoever state I am, therewith to be content" (Philippians 4:11). He was not saying that we should be thankful *for* difficulties, but to be thankful and content *despite* them. He knew that you cannot proclaim faith and belief while simultaneously being negative, critical, and worried.

Maintaining a positive frame of mind is an integral expression of faith. No matter what challenges you face today, rejoice because the Word says that "the joy of the Lord is our strength" (Nehemiah 8:10). Your life will become a glorious witness to the awesome power of the Lord who has overcome it all.

Father God, I can do all things through Your Son, Jesus Christ, who strengthens me. I am determined to stop saying words of despair and defeat and to stop looking at my world with negative eyes. I receive every benefit won for me by the shed blood of the Cross, including, salvation, healing, deliverance, and being made perfectly whole. Thank You, Father, for Your great love for me and the awesome sacrifice of Your Son so that I can walk in total victory. In the mighty name of my Lord Jesus Christ, I pray, Amen.

†

DAY 78
THE PROMISE COMES BY FAITH

Therefore, the promise comes by faith, so that it may be by grace and may be guaranteed to all Abraham's offspring – not only to those who are of the law but also to those who are of the faith of Abraham. He is the father of us all. As it is written: "I have made you a father of many nations."

He is our father in the sight of God, in whom he believed – the God who gives life to the dead and calls things that are not as though they were. Against all hope, Abraham in hope believed and so became the father of many nations, just as it had been said to him, "So shall your offspring be."

Without weakening in his faith, he faced the fact that his body was as good as dead – since he was about a hundred years old – and that Sarah's womb was also dead. Yet he did not waver through unbelief regarding the promise of God, but was strengthened in his faith and gave glory to God, being fully persuaded that God had power to do what he had promised. (Romans 4:16-21 New International Version)

The Lord God Almighty is the God of the impossible. Certainly, no average person would look at an elderly, childless couple and think there was the slightest possibility that they could have a child.

Fortunately, there have been, and still are, people of great faith. It is written that "Abraham in hope believed."

What God told him sounded preposterous in the natural world. But Abraham believed God anyway.

What did he have to do in order to believe? He had to look beyond the reality that he saw. He had to look beyond the appearance of things. Does that mean that he ignored the "facts" that he saw? No. Scripture tells us that without weakening in his faith, Abraham acknowledged the fact that he was nearly one hundred years old and that his wife Sarah was ninety, so far past her childbearing years that it was ridiculous to think that she could have a child. The medical facts were abundantly clear. Can you imagine a doctor's pronouncing with great authority that there was absolutely no hope?

Like Abraham, you can acknowledge the "facts" of your situation, but then give all power to God and not to the appearance of your health situation. Call things that are not as though they were, and call every cell in your body healthy and whole.

You have a better covenant than Abraham through the death and resurrection of the Lord Jesus Christ. Walk in the truth of the Cross that by the stripes of Jesus you are healed. Rejoice! Jesus has won the victory for you. So keep the faith and receive your healing.

Father God, I am an heir of Abraham, and I know that the promise comes by faith. Therefore, I focus only on the finished work of the Cross and on the knowledge that by the stripes of Jesus I am healed. I declare my faith in You as my Heavenly Father who gives life to the dead and calls things that are not as though they were. I rejoice in studying Your Word and speaking Your

Word. You are my Healer, my Deliverer, and My Savior. By Your mighty hand, I am made whole. Thank You, Father. Thank You. In Jesus' name, I pray, Amen.

† GREAT RESOURCES

Website for Support and Encouragement

GodWantsYouToBeWell.com
This is treasure-chest of articles on healing – from explanations of Christ's atonement, to the benefits of music for your healing, to tutorials on Bible study resources.

And perhaps best of all, this is a place to get personal support and prayers from like-minded believers! On this website you can share your own comments and receive encouragement from others. Also be sure to get your free sample of Scripture cards. (You can also order the full set.)

Books and Teaching CDs

1) *Sparkling Gems from the Greek*
2) *Paid in Full, An In-Depth Look at the Defining Moments of Christ's Passion*
3) *A Light in Darkness*
By Rick Renner
Renner Ministries
P.O. Box 702040, Tulsa, OK 74170-2040
918-496-3213
www.renner.org

1) *Dismantling Mammon*
2) *Healed: Once And For All*
3) *No More Curse*
4) *Releasing Seed That Produces Kingdom Dominion*
5) *Pressed Beyond Measure*
6) *Freedom Through the Anointing*
7) *Victory – What Would You Do If You Knew You Could Not Fail?*

By Pastor Tracy Harris
Harvest International Ministries
4000 Arkansas Boulevard
Texarkana, AR 71854
870-774-4446
www.experiencehim.org

1) *Authority of a Renewed Mind*
2) *Preparations for a Move of God*
3) *The Healing Library*

By Dr. Sandra Kennedy
Sandra Kennedy Ministries
2621 Washington Road, Augusta, GA 30904
706-737-4530
www.sandrakennedy.org

How to Live and Not Die
By Norvel Hayes
Norvel Hayes Ministries
P.O. Box 1379, Cleveland, TN 37364
423-476-1018

1) *You've Already Got It*
2) *Believer's Authority*
3) *A Better Way to Pray*
4) *The True Nature of God*
By Andrew Wommack
Andrew Wommack Ministries
P.O. Box 3333, Colorado Springs, CO 80934-3333
719-635-1111
www.awmi.net

1) *Atonement*
2) *You Shall Receive Power*
3) *Blessing or Curse*
4) *The Basics of Deliverance*
By Derek Prince
Derek Prince Ministries
P.O. Box 19501, Charlotte, North Carolina 28219
704-357-3556
www.derekprince.org

The Blessing of the Lord
By Kenneth Copeland
Kenneth Copeland Ministries
Fort Worth, TX 76192-0001
800-600-7395
www.kcm.org

1) *The Tongue – A Creative Force*
2) *Can Your Faith Fail?*
By Charles Capps
P.O. Box 69
England, AR 72046
501-842-2576
www.charlescapps.org

Christ the Healer
By F. F. Bosworth
1973, Fleming H. Revell, division of Baker Book House Co.

Music – Online, Downloads, CDs

www.soulkeeperradio.com
Soulkeeper Radio. Streaming peaceful Christian music that will restore, renew, and refresh your soul. While you are working on your computer, have soothing Christian music playing. This is a very special website, run by Melissa and Joe Champlion.

www.soulkeepermusic.com
A great website! The Baby Song, Free Evangelism Song, Free Music and more! Check out all the things the Champlions have available there.

Audiobooks
For *The Power of God's Word*

Audiobooks of *The Power of God's Word* are available at amazon.com, iTunes.com, and audible.com.

For full details, please visit: **PowerofGodsWord.com**.

Scripture Cards
For Each Volume of
The Power of God's Word Devotional Series

Get Scripture Cards for each volume of *The Power of God's Word*. Post your favorite Scriptures where you can see them often, and renew your mind with God's healing Word.

Every set of Scripture cards includes the Scriptures discussed in the corresponding volume of *The Power of God's Word*.

Visit: **PowerOfGodsWord.com** to order.

<h1>Books by Anne B. Buchanan</h1>

<u>From God's Heart to Mine</u>
This is a blank journal for recording the words that God speaks to you. There is a special foreword explaining the purpose and power of keeping this journal.
Available at amazon.com

<u>Christian Devotional Healing Series</u>
If you like this book from *The Power of God's Word* Christian Devotional Healing Series, then you will love the other volumes. For complete ordering information, please visit:
PowerofGodsWord.com

Get the series as:
- Paperback books from Amazon.com
- Digital e-books from Amazon Kindle.
- Digital e-books from Barnes and Nobles Nook.
- Scripture cards from PowerOfGodsWord.com.
- Audiobooks from amazon.com, iTunes.com, and audible.com.

<u>Volume 1 – *The Power of God's Word for Healing*</u>
70 daily devotions! You will learn:
- Why misunderstanding what the word "saved" means can keep you from being healed.
- Why saying sentences with "I am" can either help you recover or keep you sick.
- Why there is power for healing in communion.
- Why your words determine your health.
- And much more!

<u>Volume 2 – *The Power of God's Word for Receiving Healing*</u>
65 daily devotions! You will learn:

- Why it is critical to know the difference between facts and the truth.
- Why the unbelief of others can affect your recovery.
- How to look beyond the appearance of your ailments.
- Why not consulting God first can trap you.

<u>Volume 3 – *The Power of God's Word for Overcoming Hindrances to Healing*</u>
78 daily devotions! You will learn:

- Why misunderstanding Job will keep you sick.
- Why Paul's thorn was not sickness.
- Why suffering sickness does not glorify God.
- Why it is almost impossible to be healed if you don't do three important things.
- How to pray effective prayers instead of prayers that actually hinder your recovery.

<u>Volume 4 – *The Power of God's Word for Healthy Living*</u>
73 daily devotions! You will learn:

- Five easy habits to develop to promote your health.
- Why herbs and essential oils are God's blessings for healing.
- Three emotions that are critical for good health.
- Why it matters what music you listen to.
- Why some kinds of meditation hurt you instead of helping you.

A Gift for You

If you like this book, I would really appreciate your leaving a review for it at amazon.com. It would be a blessing for me, and I would be very grateful.

As a way to say "thank you," I have some free Scripture cards for you.

Please visit this website to receive your free Scripture cards: **PowerOfGodsWord.com/gft-three** .

End Notes

Cover photograph – "Purple Sedum" by Julie Gentry
www.publicdomainpictures.net

45870511R00134

Made in the USA
Lexington, KY
13 October 2015